CHINA VIRUS

How Justin Trudeau's Pro-Communist Ideology
is Putting Canadians in Danger

EZRA LEVANT

About Rebel News

Rebel News is a leading independent source of news, opinion and activism. Launched by Ezra Levant and a group of dedicated Rebels after the Sun News Network shut down, Rebel News's motto is "telling the other side of the story" — in Canada and across the world.

For more information about Rebel News, or more copies of this book, please visit *www.RebelNews.com*

TABLE OF CONTENTS

ACKNOWLEDGMENTS

Thank you to the team at Rebel News for getting this book to print so quickly, and to our loyal supporters.

CHAPTER 1

THE VIRUS ARRIVES — AND TRUDEAU GOES ON VACATION

On January 25th, 2020 the first known case of the Chinese coronavirus, also called COVID-19, was announced in Canada. A man in his fifties had flown into Toronto from Wuhan, China, the Ground Zero of the virus. Even though he felt sick on the plane, he walked right past Canadian border and immigration agents and went home. Later on, he called the ambulance. His wife fell ill the next day.

The government of Ontario held an emergency press conference about it — on a Saturday, almost unprecedented for a public health announcement. There was a sense of urgency to it; the terrifying virus that seemed so far away on TV was suddenly in the heart of Canada's biggest city.

But Justin Trudeau and his cabinet weren't there. And they had nothing to say. Actually, they did have something to say — at that very moment, many of Trudeau's MPs were out campaigning at celebrations for the Chinese Lunar new year, and were tweeting about their party-going. While Ontario's top public health officials were ringing the alarm about the China virus, Trudeau's government was hitting the snooze button.

Trudeau himself was on another one of his famous "personal days", according to his official itinerary,[1] even though he had just come off an astoundingly long 17-day Christmas holiday in Costa Rica, and was still sporting his vacation beard. And Chrystia Freeland, the deputy prime minister to whom Trudeau had delegated most of his ever-lighter workload, was overseas, partying with the international jet-set at the World Economic Forum in Davos[2], Switzerland. No-one was minding the store.

The next morning, Canada's Sunday newspapers were panicked; there was a giant manhunt on for thirty other passengers who had been on the same plane from China as the man who would turn out to be Canada's first case of COVID-19. But Trudeau couldn't be roused — a full day after the virus bombshell, he was still in hiding and his official itinerary was blank, other than noting he was taking another "personal day". That week, virus cases would be reported in B.C., and then Quebec, too.

On January 31st, U.S. President Donald Trump imposed restrictions on flights from China to the United States, barring non-citizens. But Trudeau would wait another six weeks, until mid-March, before making the same decision. He had other things on his mind — including another vacation, just days away.

On February 6th Trudeau left Canada and flew to Ethiopia, to start his next foreign adventure — a nine-day overseas junket, meeting with some of Africa's worst dictators, offering them massive foreign aid gifts in return for their votes for Canada to be given a temporary seat on the United Nations Security Council. A review of Trudeau's international travel schedule since he became prime minister in 2015 shows there was no period of time in which he was away from Canada more than he was during those crucial first weeks of the pandemic.

That doesn't mean he wasn't thinking about it — or shedding one of his famous tears for the cameras. When Trudeau was in Ethiopia

---

1   *https://pm.gc.ca/en/news/itineraries/2020/01/25/prime-ministers-itinerary-saturday-january-25-2020*

2   *https://pm.gc.ca/en/news/itineraries/2020/01/24/deputy-prime-ministers-itinerary-saturday-january-25-2020*

on February 9ᵗʰ, he made a grandiose gesture to the victims of the virus. He ordered Canada's national stockpile of face masks, gloves and doctors' scrubs to be gathered up— sixteen tons of personal protection equipment.

And he put them on a plane to China.

For free.

To one of the largest, richest countries in the world.

The dictatorship that is still holding two Canadian hostages.

And he boasted about it.

"Canada supports China's ongoing response to novel coronavirus outbreak", was the headline[3] on the Liberal press release, signed by Trudeau's foreign minister. "This is vital to helping those affected and protecting the health and safety of people around the world."

The virus was racing through Canada; it was pouring into our country every day, on unrestricted flights from China. And Trudeau just gave away our national stockpile of medical equipment.

Those first few weeks showed a pattern: Justin Trudeau's personal laziness and inattentiveness; combined with his deference to so-called experts, including the World Health Organization (WHO); and all of it coloured by Trudeau's globalist ideology of open borders and submissiveness to Communist China.

By June, the virus had killed more than 8,000 Canadians — mercifully not tens of thousands, or even hundreds of thousands as some public health "experts" had predicted. But the crisis revealed many things about Trudeau that we had only seen flashes of before. It showed how beholden to foreign interests Trudeau and his Liberals had become and how, time and again, Trudeau chose to obey or even copy Communist China as a role model. It showed an authoritarian streak in Trudeau — how he used the China virus as an excuse to weaken Canada's Parliament, to reduce our civil liberties and to rack up more debt in two months than Canada did in two world wars.

It showed that Trudeau really meant it when he once told Liberal donors "there's a level of admiration I actually have for China because

---

3   *https://www.canada.ca/en/global-affairs/news/2020/02/canada-supports-chinas-ongoing-response-to-novel-coronavirus-outbreak.html*

[of] their basic dictatorship." He wasn't just obedient to the Chinese Communist Party. In important ways, he wanted to emulate it.

That's what this book is about. The China virus caught many countries off guard (but not all). Some world leaders have risen to the occasion, some haven't. But very few have made every possible mistake, and chosen every wrong choice. And in the end, Trudeau's disastrous pro-Beijing ideology has put Canadians in greater danger than even the virus itself.

CHAPTER 2

A LIGHTWEIGHT PM IN HEAVY TIMES

Justin Trudeau doesn't pay attention to details at the best of times. When he was caught taking his family on a secret, free vacation to "Billionaire Island" in the Bahamas, owned by the Aga Khan, a man who lobbies the Canadian government for millions of dollars in grants, Trudeau made the most astonishing defence of his actions. Trudeau was being investigated by the Conflict of Interest and Ethics Commissioner for it, and he had an excuse that sounds like he came up with it himself: Taking a secret payment from a businessman who gets federal government grants couldn't have been a conflict of interest, you see, because Trudeau never pays any attention to the details of government business. Trudeau simply couldn't have been corrupted by the six-figure gift of a private island vacation, because if the Aga Khan had tried to turn it into a quid pro quo, Trudeau simply wouldn't have known what anyone was talking about! He was in the dark.

That was his legal defence, according to Mary Dawson, the judge who convicted Trudeau of breaking the law. Here's how she summed up[4] Trudeau's approach to governing: "He said his role in any meeting is to further develop a relationship between the individual and Canada. Mr. Trudeau views his involvement with the Aga Khan and his Canadian institutions as ceremonial in nature, similar to interactions he would have with any global leader or distinguished global citizen."

Trudeau told Dawson he doesn't even regard his meetings as "business" — all the hard parts are done by other staff before or after he does his schmoozing. "The meetings he attends as Prime Minister are not business meetings. Rather, they are high-level meetings centred on relationship building and ensuring that all parties are moving forward together. Specific issues or details are worked out before, subsequently or independently of any meeting he attends," she wrote in her ruling.

The long-standing Conservative Party criticism of Trudeau as being shallow ("nice hair, though") isn't even an insult. It's what Trudeau thinks of himself — he's just there to take selfies with adoring fans, and make Zoolander male-model poses for the cameras. After "social distancing" became a thing, he simply took to reading a prepared script at a daily press conference, before going back into Rideau Cottage, never to be seen for the rest of the day.

What was that all about — the months of "self-hiding"? Trudeau's estranged wife, Sophie, flew to London, U.K., on a junket and contracted the virus, and apparently gave it to British sex symbol Idris Elba while she was over there. Upon her return, she quarantined herself, living at the summer cottage property provided by the government for the prime minister, at Harrington Lake, in Quebec.

But why did Trudeau himself choose to quarantine himself — for a period of much longer than the two weeks the virus could remain latent? Trudeau didn't have any symptoms; if he did, he could have immediately been tested for the virus, as Donald Trump was (Trump's test came back negative) or the U.K.'s Boris Johnson (the test came back positive, and Johnson was eventually hospitalized).

Why would Trudeau sentence himself to a quarantine without any symptoms — and stay in quarantine so long? Why wouldn't he simply be tested, and go back to work immediately?

---

4   *https://ciec-ccie.parl.gc.ca/en/publications/Documents/InvestigationReports/The%20Trudeau%20Report.pdf*

Well, the question answers itself — taking the test would confirm what we all know (and what Trudeau obviously knew): he didn't have the virus, and if he took the test, he wouldn't have any fig leaf of an excuse for holing up all day in his 22-room mansion. He loved it — an excuse to stay home. No cabinet meetings, no commanding the ship of state. As he told the Ethics Commissioner: any real work is done by other people, anyways. He's more about the "relationships" and the "ceremonies". And, besides, he was still in vacation mode — he still had his vacation beard left over from his 17-day Costa Rican bender, and he obviously needed another holiday to recover from his African adventure. Canada's laziest prime minister just wanted to be able to watch Netflix all day and smoke legal marijuana, and now he had an excuse of sorts.

Trudeau quarantined himself when there was no medical or legal reason to do so — he just wanted to have some personal time. But when leaving the house became subject to legal restrictions, when various provinces and cities were enacting emergency health legislation to lock down the country, that's when Trudeau decided he was ready to leave his home.

Health authorities across Canada asked that Canadians not visit their country homes or summer cottages; national and provincial parks were closed; and some provinces even set up check-stops along their borders. The most extreme "social distancing" moment in Canada happened to coincide with the Easter weekend, a time when families traditionally gathered together in churches or at homes. That was the moment when, according to public health officials, the danger was the highest.

And yet that was the one moment when Trudeau himself decided he was ready to leave his self-imposed house arrest and venture out into the world. Not to his job — in Parliament, or at the cabinet table. But to visit Sophie, and the kids who had been living with her at the government's Harrington Lake property in Quebec's lovely Gatineau Park.

Except that broke at least four different rules — rules that Trudeau had just hectored Canadians about in his daily press statement. No travelling from Ontario to Quebec; no going into a federal park; no going to the country house; no mixing households. Perhaps Trudeau himself knew just how bad it would look if word got out, so he didn't have his personal photographer publicize the trip. After all, Scotland's chief public health officer had just resigned in disgrace after police gave her a caution, for driving around the country[5] with her family on a road trip in the middle of the lock-down she had just ordered. New Zealand's health minister was demoted[6] after going to the beach on the first weekend after he told citizens that wasn't allowed. But not Trudeau; the rules are for the little people, not him. The police wouldn't caution Trudeau, like police did to the Scottish politician — the police actually escorted him as he broke the rules. And lucky for Trudeau, he himself was the prime minister — so there was no-one to demote him from cabinet. But who was even to know about it, if Trudeau didn't tell the world in a tweet? And he didn't. But Sophie — the same grifter who mooched the free vacation on Billionaire Island in the Bahamas — just couldn't help herself, posting glamour shots of the whole family on Instagram,[7] like a low-rent Kardashian. "Even though families across the country are having to get a little creative and celebrate a bit differently this year, we're all in this together. So whether you're able to be with your loved ones or you're staying connected from afar, we're thinking of you and keeping you in our hearts," she wrote.

Well, that's the thing. The Trudeau family didn't have to celebrate a bit differently, did they? And Sophie Trudeau wanted you to know it. And in a perfect Marie Antoinette moment when called out on it — a rare moment of indignation from the Media Party — Trudeau laughed.

He had literally just scolded Canadians for wanting to visit with their families — he had told[8] them before the Easter weekend to "stay home" and "Skype that big family dinner". But when pressed for why he didn't just do that, too, it was like he couldn't even understand the question. It was him, Justin Trudeau. Why would he follow the rules

---

5   *https://www.bbc.com/news/uk-scotland-52177171*

6   *https://www.theguardian.com/world/2020/apr/07/new-zealand-health-minister-demoted-after-beach-visit-broke-lockdown-rules*

7   *https://www.instagram.com/p/B-5bgxkl33G/?hl=en*

8   *https://globalnews.ca/news/6815936/coronavirus-justin-trudeau-andrew-scheer-easter-travel/*

he just laid out for others? "After three weeks of my family living up at Harrington and me working here, I went to join them for Easter weekend. We continue to follow all the instructions from public health authorities," he said. Except that was exactly what was against the rules — the rules he had just announced. Even Ottawa's subsidized press corps had to challenge him. "Yes, but did somebody tell you this was OK?" asked one journalist. "All over social media, people are wondering why this exception was OK for you, why it was OK for you to go see your family at the cottage?" Bold questions from a normally submissive press gallery; the blinking look of incomprehension from Trudeau said it all. It was like a commoner was asking the prince why he wears a crown. "My family has been living there for three weeks," Trudeau said. "This is where my wife and my children live."

Just be grateful he didn't fly down to the Bahamas again.

Trudeau made a daily press statement for the first months of the pandemic, just like many provincial premiers, big-city mayors and of course the master of the press conference, Donald Trump, who would sometimes hold court for up to two hours a day. Unlike Trump, though, Trudeau carefully screened the list of journalists permitted to attend, allowing only journalistic outlets deemed "trustworthy" — keeping out conservative or skeptical journalists like Rebel News and other critics. But whereas Trump and Canada's premiers often had team-style briefings with public health experts and captains of industry, Trudeau didn't — at the height of the crisis he simply read a statement and gave vague answers to any questions that were deeper than the ceremonial clichés that he sees as his job description. There were other briefings by federal experts — including Canada's Chief Public Health Officer, Dr. Theresa Tam, and the Health Minister, Patty Hajdu. But Trudeau didn't bother to attend them — he was self-hiding.

But by hiving himself off from those briefings, Trudeau managed to decouple himself from political responsibility for any decisions. As usual, he simply deferred to those advisors, and accepted whatever their advice was — applying no judgment of his own. Trudeau repeatedly said he simply follows the advice of experts — by late March he was clearly running out of patience with anyone who questioned his advice. "I am going to make sure that we continue to follow all recommendations of public health officers," he said. It was an appeal to authority — if you disagreed with him, you were obviously anti-science. But it was also Trudeau putting down a marker that if things go bad, he'd have someone else to blame.

The trouble with that is, experts are only experts in their field — in medicine, in epidemics — but it's the prime minister's job to listen to those experts, and balance them with other considerations — like the contrary advice of other experts, like his own assessment of the credibility of experts dealing with an unknown problem. Scientists don't all agree; science is not settled. And then there are non-medical considerations, like the economy and civil liberties.

Truly great leaders try to break up groupthink; Abraham Lincoln famously appointed to his cabinet three of his own political rivals who had run against him for president. Not Trudeau — he'd find an "expert" opinion and just rubber-stamp it. But even an expert who's right about his area of expertise can be wrong when the national interest is considered — a virus can be deadly, but so can another Great Depression; so can the loss of personal liberty. And then there's the consideration that the ultimate source of "expert" opinion followed by both Tam and Hajdu is that of the World Health Organization (WHO), a United Nations agency dominated by Communist China, that has been complicit with China's propaganda falsifying key facts about the virus.

When Trudeau deferred to expert opinion, he certainly didn't mean Hajdu — the gender-quota Health Minister whose profession before politics was as a graphic designer. Hajdu replaced Dr. Jane Philpott, the accomplished physician widely regarded as Trudeau's most competent cabinet minister, until she was fired for supporting Jody Wilson-Raybould, the Justice Minister sacked by Trudeau for opposing his sweetheart deal to subvert the justice system on behalf of the corrupt Quebec engineering firm of SNC Lavalin.

For Trudeau, listening to the experts really meant listening to Theresa Tam; and Tam is not only deferential to the WHO, she still sits on their Oversight and Advisory Committee[9] to this day. How could she dissent from the WHO, when she works for the WHO?

---

9   *https://www.who.int/about/who_reform/emergency-capacities/oversight-committee/members/en/*

Tam's advice perfectly matched that of the WHO — which meant whatever they got wrong, she got wrong.

So, for example, the WHO adopted China's point of view that criticism of China or restricting travellers from China was a form of racism. And lo and behold, Tam's first major pronouncement on the virus — on January 29th, just days after the first case in Ontario — was to condemn as racists any Canadians who were worried about the virus.

"I am concerned about the growing number of reports of racism and stigmatizing comments on social media directed to people of Chinese and Asian descent related to coronavirus," she said.[10] "End stigma."

But there hadn't been any reports of anti-Chinese racism, and Tam couldn't provide any examples. There had been some online petitions[11] from parents asking that their children's schools provide face masks in class, and that recent travellers from China quarantine themselves. But the petitions were not racial; they were related to genuine risk factors. And the petition campaigners themselves were often Asian, like Erjun Li, who collected more than 10,000 signatures in Ontario's York Region. He's clearly not anti-Asian — he's Chinese himself. As Asian-Canadian journalist Ian Young argues,[12] one of the reasons why Vancouver's virus contagion was less than other Canadian cities, especially given the city's travel ties to China, is precisely because they weren't hung up on political correctness. "Credit goes to a shrewd Chinese community, which was socially distancing long before others had heard of the term, and long after well-meaning folk told them to stop being so silly about this 'pandemic' thing," he wrote.

But not Tam — she was fully invested in the racism narrative. Her press briefing that day in January claimed to be about public health. But her prescription was a dose of identity politics. "Help stop the spread of biases", she said. "Don't make assumptions about people or use stereotypes. Be careful of the language you use. Go to trusted and verified information sites."

---

10   *https://twitter.com/CPHO_Canada/status/1222704579172864002*

11   *https://www.ipetitions.com/petition/stop-2019nCoV-spread-in-york-region-school*

12   *https://twitter.com/ianjamesyoung70/status/1247640036968783873*

By the way, none of that is medical advice. That's political advice. More precisely, that's a political accusation, an attack. If you're worried about the virus, you're a racist — even if you're Chinese-Canadian yourself. This was a classic Liberal Party move — attack your potential critics first, put them on the back foot by implying that any criticism of Canada's non-preparation was racist. It was used as an excuse to resist recommending masks and quarantines, just as it was used in Canada's ongoing debate about open, unguarded borders — no mainstream media, no Conservative politician, dares to criticize open-border immigration, because they'll be called racist. A pandemic thrives on open borders, so the tactic was a natural fit: if you're worried about the pandemic, you're a racist. That was Tam's first statement, her debut into the whole crisis.

Yet it was Chinese-Canadians who were the most scared — because they had been following the Chinese epidemic the most closely. They're the ones who stayed away from the Chinese stores and malls in Canada. It wasn't racism. Chinese people aren't racist against Chinese malls. They were afraid of the virus. Theresa Tam had no advice for them, nothing useful — other than to stop asking questions. Shut up, she explained. She was the perfect hire as Trudeau's public health scold.

But she's a doctor, so she did have a prescription:[13] She thought Canadians needed to police our language. Funny; that's what the Wuhan police said to people concerned about the virus too.

"Racism, discrimination and stigmatizing language are unacceptable and very hurtful. These actions create a divide of us vs them. Canada is a country built on the deep-rooted values of respect, diversity and inclusion," said Tam.

When Tam started her daily briefings, she was a bit of a media darling. But after two months of platitudes, even the normally submissive Ottawa press gallery was starting to get restless.

For example, Tam bizarrely spent weeks publicly claiming that wearing masks was not only unnecessary, but actually dangerous — a position parroted by Hajdu and Trudeau, despite it being the universal public practice in countries like Taiwan and Singapore, a practice that kept those countries' death tolls from the virus to single digits, despite

---

13   *https://twitter.com/CPHO_Canada/status/1222705113669799938*

their close connections to China. No matter; Tam would say it daily: "Putting a mask on an asymptomatic person is not beneficial," she said as late as March 30th.[14] "The scientific evidence is that if you are sick then put on a mask to prevent those droplets from flying in any space as you are going to a clinic or move yourself around the community for essential needs."

But even a non-expert can see that's wrong. The whole point of the 14-day quarantine is that someone with the virus can show no symptoms — that's what asymptomatic means — for two weeks, while still being able to infect other people. Other viruses like Ebola[15] aren't contagious until the victim has symptoms. The trouble with the Chinese coronavirus is that victims without obvious symptoms can spread it for up to two weeks before they even know they're sick. It's precisely those people that the masks are made for. Why would Tam say the opposite?

Anyone who knows it's better to cough into your arm than to cough into the air can intuit that it's better to wear a mask than to wear none. So why would Tam go the extra mile to positively denounce mask-wearing — to say it's actually dangerous? Masks give "a false sense of confidence," she claimed, without citing any scientific studies on the matter. "People are not protecting their eyes or other aspects where the virus enters your body," she said.

Wearing goggles or a visor may be a good idea too; or it may be a bit much. But how is that an argument for not wearing a mask? Oh, but she was on a warpath against masks: "The outside of a mask could be contaminated. The key is hand washing. Even in the hospital setting, we find that it's removing personal protective equipment that can actually lead to infection."

Huh? At most, that's a call to throw out masks at the end of the day. But surely if a mask was contaminated during the day, not wearing that mask would have meant the virus would be in your nose or mouth instead. Again, there was no science cited here.

Why?

---

14   *https://nowtoronto.com/lifestyle/coronavirus-who-should-wear-face-masks/*

15   *https://www.who.int/emergencies/diseases/ebola/frequently-asked-questions*

Well, look no further than the grand expert to which all the experts defer. There was a chain of obedience: Trudeau obeying Tam, and Tam obeying the World Health Organization. But the trouble is, the WHO lied — because they themselves deferred to the Chinese Communist Party, which was in full cover-up mode, for face-saving propaganda, but also to buy China time — time to hoover up hundreds of millions of masks, respirators, gloves and gowns from the whole world before Europe, America and Australia became alarmed and started thinking about masks, too. Back to that in a moment.

CHAPTER 3

CHINA COVERS UP ITS CHERNOBYL

Here's what the World Health Organization was saying in mid-January — taking the Chinese Communist Party's word at face value. On January 12th, they issued this advice: "At this stage, there is no clear evidence of human-to-human transmission in the novel coronavirus (2019-nC0V) outbreak in Wuhan, China. However, the Chinese authorities continue intensive surveillance and follow-up measures, including environmental investigations."

And two days later, another announcement, also trusting the Chinese government: "Preliminary investigations conducted by the Chinese authorities have found no clear evidence of human-to-human transmission of the novel coronavirus (2019-nCoV) identified in Wuhan, China."

That was a complete lie. It wasn't even still a secret lie. Incredibly, on January 1st, 2020, China's Xinhua News Agency[16] boasted that police

---

16   *https://translate.google.com/translate?sl=auto&tl=en&u =http%3A%2F%2Fwww.xinhuanet.com%2F2020-01%2F01%2Fc_1125412773. htm*

21

arrested eight doctors in Wuhan for spreading "false information" about the "Wuhan Viral Pneumonia".

The doctors were whistleblowers — and were seeking advice from their colleagues. Not only did the Chinese police arrest and punish them, they published the Chinese Communist Party's own official version of the medical science: "Some medical institutions in Wuhan have found and received multiple cases of pneumonia... However, some netizens publish and forward false information on the Internet without verification, causing adverse social impact."

So the police weren't just silencing the whistleblowers. They were creating their own, alternative version of the medical truth. "After investigation and verification by the public security organs, eight illegal personnel have been summoned and handled according to law." So it wasn't even a medical investigation. It was a police investigation.

This is the authority the WHO relied on; that Theresa Tam then relied on; that Patty Hajdu relied on; and that Justin Trudeau relied on.

And the Wuhan police had a warning for anyone who dared to cross them: "Wuhan police reminded that laws and regulations should be followed when posting information and remarks on the Internet. The police will investigate and deal with illegal acts of fabricating, spreading rumours and disrupting social order, and will not tolerate them." That was a warning to any would-be whistleblowers: if you talk about the virus, you'll be arrested for "disrupting the social order". The police — that is, the Chinese Communist Party — simply declared that the virus was no problem, and threatened anyone who disagreed with arrest. Remember, said the police, "build a harmonious and clear cyberspace." Nothing about honesty or transparency, nothing about health, actually. Just political hygiene — be silent, submissive and obedient.

And here's the key lie — the lie repeated by the WHO for more than a month: "After consultation with experts on viral pneumonia, as of the 31st [of December, 2019], no human-to-human transmission was found in the investigation, and no medical staff infection was found."

That's a lie. A deadly lie that gave all the ammunition to the "experts" like Tam and Hajdu — and thus, to Trudeau — to keep our airports open to flights from China, including from Wuhan, for months to come.

Like with Chernobyl, we'll have to wait until the Chinese Communist Party is gone before knowing the truth about the virus. But it is hard to ignore a striking coincidence: the city of Wuhan, the source of the epidemic, just happens to be the city where the only high security virus research lab in all of China is located — the Wuhan Institute of Virology. For years, China had boasted about the lab, and its peculiar practice of sending out virus hunters into caves around China to harvest bats and the small tics that live on them. Just last year, the Chinese government broadcast[17] a ten-minute promotional video showing their bat hunter going into caves, putting up nets over the mouths of the caves, and flushing out the bats within for capture.

The video made that virologist, Tian Junhua, look like a hero, and even emphasized the grave danger he was in. But the risk was worth it, they said — the last scene in the propaganda film is a boast that in the past 200 years, scientists in the entire world had only discovered 2,284 different viruses, but China has discovered 2,000 in just the past 12 years. China was very proud of this — it was a virus superpower.

Was that virus lab the source of the pandemic? Two Chinese researchers in Wuhan published a scientific paper[18] on the subject in February, showing just how close Wuhan's two virus labs were to the Huanan Seafood Market, where allegedly the virus had leapt from bats to people. Except the two researchers claimed to have interviewed 59 people in Wuhan who frequented that "wet" market, and every single one of them said they simply didn't sell bats there. After causing a bit of a stir, the study was un-published, as things sometimes are in China.

So did it come from at wet market, or from a government "research" lab? We don't know. But, incredibly, Canada has a history of involvement with Wuhan's virus industry that would shock most Canadians.

---

17   *https://youtu.be/tRuw3lWQpis*

18   *https://img-prod.tgcom24.mediaset.it/images/2020/02/16/114720192-5eb8307f-017c-4075-a697-348628da0204.pdf*

In October, 2019 — a month before the pandemic claimed its first victim — an incredible story[19] broke: a Chinese citizen was fired from a Canadian lab after sending secrets to Wuhan. Here's how the CBC reported it back then: "A Canadian government scientist at the National Microbiology Lab in Winnipeg made at least five trips to China in 2017-18, including one to train scientists and technicians at China's newly certified Level 4 lab, which does research with the most deadly pathogens."

Xiangguo Qiu was frog-marched out of the Winnipeg lab by the RCMP. She had been making regular trips to Wuhan's virus lab, spending two weeks at a time there.

She was allegedly spying — and maybe more.

But then there's an even stranger story[20] about Canadian viruses: Justin Trudeau just plain old gave the Chinese Communist Party some of the most deadly viruses in the world, that had been securely held in that same Winnipeg lab. No need to steal it — just call up Trudeau, and he'll ship it right over.

"'I think the Chinese activities… are highly suspicious,' one expert said, after it was revealed a Winnipeg lab sent samples of Ebola and henipavirus to China," reported the *National Post* in August of 2019.

Everyone has heard of Ebola — one of the most deadly and contagious viruses ever known, a disease with a fatality rate exceeding 50%. But henipaviruses? That's a fancy way of saying fruit bat viruses.

Why was Trudeau sending those to China? To the very same Wuhan lab?

Taiwan — the victim of Chinese viruses and virus-cover-ups — wanted to know. A headline[21] in the Taiwan News last August read, "Canada may have assisted China's bio-warfare program with transfer of lethal viruses".

It's clear that Taiwan was expecting the worst from China — and placed no trust in the World Health Organization, from which it was

19   *https://www.cbc.ca/news/canada/manitoba/national-microbiology-lab-scientist-investigation-china-1.5307424*

20   *https://nationalpost.com/health/bio-warfare-experts-question-why-canada-was-sending-lethal-viruses-to-china*

21   *https://www.taiwannews.com.tw/en/news/3761093*

expelled, at China's demand. "A startling report from Canada… reveals that Canadian health officials approved the transfer of dangerous virus samples to China in March of 2019, which could potentially be used to advance a dangerous bio-warfare program in the secretive communist state.

"Officials from Canada's National Microbiology Laboratory (NML) have defended the transfer of Henipavirus and Ebola samples as part of an international public health research campaign. However, experts in the field are raising alarm about the transfer, which is now reportedly at the centre of a government investigation by the Royal Canadian Mounted Police (RCMP)."

What possible good could have come from that? Why did Canada see fit to make itself the source of the world's worst viruses for China — was it because other western countries with access to that deadly material were less cooperative with China? And — just like China hides the truth — would the Canadian government ever admit it if our bat viruses were involved in the COVID-19 outbreak?

Perhaps it was possible before this pandemic for the most naive — and wilfully blind — prime minister in the world to think that sending deadly viruses to a top security Chinese research lab was a good idea. But it takes a special level of carelessness or malice to support that same lab after the pandemic broke.

In a scoop uncovered by Rebel News's Sheila Gunn Reid, Justin Trudeau did just that. On March 6th, 2020, Trudeau approved[22] an $828,000 grant to that very same Wuhan Institute of Virology to study the virus. Some of the grant would go to Canadian researchers. But it would be led by China:[23] "our team members in Wuhan who currently perform the standard diagnostic tests will lead this effort," read the grant proposal.

As Gunn pointed out, even if the Wuhan virus lab wasn't the centre of RCMP investigations for industrial espionage, it's just plain sloppy. U.S. diplomatic and scientific officials visited the site and sent cables

---

22   *https://www.canada.ca/en/institutes-health-research/news/2020/03/government-of-canada-invests-27m-in-coronavirus-research--details-of-the-funded-projects.html*

23   *https://www.rebelnews.com/trudeau_research_grant_nearly_one_million_dollars_covid19_research_wuhan_virus_research_laboratory*

back to the U.S. "warning about safety and management weaknesses at the WIV lab and proposed more attention and help. The first cable also warns that the lab's work on bat coronaviruses and their potential human transmission represented a risk of a new SARS-like pandemic."

Was it sloppiness or was it deliberate? Who knows — literally. Who would ever be able to say? Would the Chinese nationals getting the $838,000 payday from Trudeau even be able to report honestly back to Canada what they were doing?

And why was Trudeau taking Canadian tax dollars and sending them to China as a sort of foreign aid, to begin with? China is next only to the U.S. in terms of economic clout; it has US$3 trillion in foreign reserves — it doesn't need $838,000 from Canada. It can fund its biohazards or bioweapons on its own. But imagine doing that — giving a gift to China; to the same virus lab; after the pandemic — all while China still holds two Canadians hostage.

That $838,000 isn't going to cure the virus.

It's not going to do anything other than to cement in the minds of the Chinese Communist Party that they can literally do anything — kidnap two Canadians; kill thousands more with disease — and Justin Trudeau will still give them close to a million dollars without them even asking for it.

CHAPTER 4

WHOSE SIDE IS WHO ON?

Unbeknownst to most people, while the WHO was telling the world publicly that there was little to no risk, there was actually a battle raging[24] within the WHO about whether or not to tell the truth, and declare a global health emergency — a "public health emergency of international concern" as it's technically called.

The debate raged for days within the WHO, but the agency was deadlocked — China insisted the virus wasn't contagious, but other countries' doctors insisted it was. According to the *Guardian* newspaper, "China argued against declaring an emergency on 22 January, but could not have carried the argument alone... for the vote to have been split, several western, or western-aligned, representatives must have voted with Beijing."

Only 15 countries in the world had a representative on that committee, called the "IHR Emergency Committee for the COVID-19 outbreak". Only 15 countries, and Canada was one of them. And Canada's representative was Theresa Tam.[25]

---

24   *https://www.theguardian.com/world/2020/apr/18/caught-in-a-superpower-struggle-the-inside-story-of-the-whos-response-to-coronavirus*

25   *https://www.who.int/ihr/procedures/EC_COVID_19_Biographies_Final.pdf?ua=1*

How countries voted is apparently a secret — like so much of what the WHO and other UN agencies do. But neither alternative is any good.

If Tam voted along with China to lie, and to continue to falsely claim that the virus wasn't contagious from person to person, she was a party to one of the deadliest public health decisions in recent times.

But if she voted against China, and for disclosure of the truth — and was blocked by China — it's in some ways worse. She would have known how bad it was; she would have seen, first-hand, how China was manipulating and blocking the facts, corrupting the science. And yet she still parroted the WHO line in public, and other deceptions. Because — even today — she remains an employee of the WHO.

You don't need to have attended that January debate at the WHO to know that the Chinese Communist Party lies. You don't need to be an expert or a doctor. In fact, the plainer you are, the more obvious it is — Communist dictatorships lie. The Soviet Union lied about the Chernobyl nuclear disaster, because they didn't want to show weakness to the west, and certainly not to their own people. There are lies within lies — in a culture where disagreement and dissent are banned, people lie to each other, and even to the dictator; no-one wants to tell him the bad news. It's essential that a tyrant appears to be infallible. But the Wuhan biological Chernobyl was much worse than the explosion of the Soviet version. Chernobyl was an economic and political disaster that helped bring down the Soviet Union. But by nature, it posed a risk mainly to those geographically close to it — Ukraine, Belarus, and Russia (now independent countries). Despite the spectacular explosion, fewer than 100 people died, either from the blast or its radiation aftermath. By contrast, the virus from Wuhan had spread to more than 4 million people in 185 countries by June, and the death toll was nearly 500,000 — and likely many more hidden by suppressed Chinese statistics, too.

It wouldn't be the first time China lied to itself, and to the world. Even now, China's official position[26] is that it didn't kill a single protester at Tiananmen Square, a bloody massacre in 1989 where an estimated 10,000 democracy protesters were murdered by 200,000

---

26   *http://www.chinadaily.com.cn/opinion/2011-07/14/content_12898720.htm*

Chinese troops. If China's government still brazenly denies that, how could anyone trust them about virus statistics? Well, that's why the World Health Organization was so valuable to China — it laundered China's own propaganda, through the good name of "public health".

But even pro-China fools like Trudeau's cabinet should have known better. They were certainly warned often enough. U.S. intelligence agencies have reported that China was lying about the true extent of the virus. Leaked documents from Germany's national intelligence agency show that China's president Xi Jinping personally phoned[27] the WHO's Tedros Adhanom on January 21, asking the agency to delay reporting that the virus was contagious from person to person. And Canada's own medical intelligence unit of the Canadian Forces raised the same concerns — also back in January.[28] But not only did Tam continue to parrot China's WHO propaganda, Patty Hajdu positively attacked anyone who challenged the official stats, calling them conspiracy theorists!

"There's no indication that the data that came out of China in terms of their infection rate and their death rate was falsified in any way," she angrily told reporters on April 2nd, long after the rest of the world had realized they were being fed Chernobyl-style propaganda from China, via the WHO. "Your question is feeding into conspiracy theories that many people have been perpetuating on the Internet," she added — tracking the language of the Wuhan police when they arrested the eight whistle-blowing doctors.

It wasn't just that Hajdu believed China's spin. It's that she rededicated herself to collaborating with the Chinese dictatorship, insisting that Canada remain loyal to them and their WHO guidance. "No way to beat a global pandemic if we're actually not willing to work together as a globe." Except the countries that really did beat the pandemic — Taiwan, South Korea, Singapore, and the city of Hong Kong — ignored the disinformation of the WHO, and put up borders and quarantines in defiance of China. More than two months after the

---

27   *https://nypost.com/2020/05/10/china-pressured-who-to-delay-global-coronavirus-warning/*

28   *https://www.cbc.ca/news/politics/coronavirus-pandemic-covid-canadian-military-intelligence-wuhan-1.5528381*

virus arrived in Canada, Hajdu was still fiercely loyal to the Chinese public health edicts, despite their failure to keep Canadians safe.

Such loyalty is rare — and it didn't go unnoticed. Chen Weihua, a Communist Party operative at the *People's Daily* newspaper, took the unusual step of praising Hajdu publicly. "Canadian Health Minister Hajdu is a role model.[29] She is a disappointment to those paparazzi journalists and fearmongers," he tweeted. There's nothing more clunky than praise and condemnation written in Beijing and translated into English — calling Canada's tame Parliamentary Press Gallery "paparazzi" is one of the few insults they don't deserve; and calling Hajdu, the least-qualified health minister in memory, a "role model" is just too laughable to be taken seriously if it were written by a real journalist. But Chen Weihua isn't a real journalist — despite being accredited by Trudeau and the official Press Gallery — and the *People's Daily* isn't a real newspaper. They're agents of the Chinese Communist Party. In fact, Chen's tweet was the most succinct proof that indeed Hajdu was parroting Chinese propaganda — he couldn't have been more condescending had he walked up to her and patted her on the head.

That slavish submission to China wasn't limited to Trudeau's cabinet. Trudeau's CBC state broadcaster amplified the Chinese embassy's talking points on a daily basis — especially in those key first weeks, when the WHO was lying, and the virus was spreading around the world.

On January 25th, literally the same day the first patient was announced in Canada, the CBC published a story that can only be called political disinformation, claiming that concern about the virus was simply fear being whipped up by the Internet — exactly the same language used by the Wuhan police.

"'It plays to our worst fears': Coronavirus misinformation fuelled by social media", the CBC reported.[30] "Experts say social media has increased the spread of misinformation during outbreaks". And take a look at what the CBC said was misinformation: "People collapsing

---

29   *https://twitter.com/chenweihua/status/1245987548717035520*

30   *https://www.cbc.ca/news/health/coronavirus-canada-social-media-misinformation-1.5440334*

in the streets of Wuhan, coverups of unreported deaths and travellers 'escaping' quarantine in China at risk of spreading the coronavirus. If you've been following the outbreak on social media, you may have seen some, or more, of these types of claims. But the truth is, they're completely unverified – and in most cases, flat out untrue."

Except all of those things were absolutely true — and so much worse. Even the CBC's argument was bizarre: they claimed that those Internet rumours were unverified (despite hundreds of cell phone videos being shared online by desperate Wuhan citizens). But in the next breath they claimed those stories were "flat out untrue". Well, which is it — untrue, or just uncheckable because of Chinese censorship?

No matter; like Patty Hajdu's bizarre rant, the CBC was just parroting China's state broadcasters, and for the same reason: to please their boss.

So that was what the official people said — the official health experts, the official media and the official politicians. It was all overblown, Internet rumours; and there was no need to close borders or wear masks.

As the weeks went by, that advice clearly did not hold up — the virus had spread throughout the world and into Canada. The WHO changed their line, a bit. Now they were saying that wearing masks made sense for doctors, but not for the public. In language that was clearly parroted by Theresa Tam and other WHO disciples, there was a peculiar attempt to demonize the use of masks on a widespread basis: "In community settings, medical masks are not recommended for people without symptoms. For those who choose to wear medical masks, appropriate mask management should be followed, which includes how to use and dispose of masks."[31] The day after that statement, Trudeau approved the shipment of Canada's mask stockpile to China.

Why would China have wanted those masks so badly if they didn't work?

Did the WHO's advice play a role in Trudeau giving away our precious national stockpile?

---

31   *https://www.who.int/docs/default-source/coronavirus/situation-reports/20200208-sitrep-19-ncov.pdf?sfvrsn=6e091ce6_2*

Were there any contrary opinions expressed around the cabinet table? By whom — Patty Hajdu, the graphic designer sitting in the Health Minister's seat?

That incoherence continued until April. On March 26th, the WHO published an instructional video positively warning against masks. "If you do not have any respiratory symptoms, such as fever, cough, or runny nose, you do not need to wear a medical mask. When used alone, masks can give you a false feeling of protection and can even be a source[32] of infection when not used correctly."

How could that happen? And why did Trudeau's CBC state broadcaster echo the bizarre claim that masks were positively dangerous? In one[33] typical story, CBC's Indigenous bureau wrote about a Metis woman who had started making masks with beadwork — not only useful and beautiful, but an expression of her culture. Normally that's something the CBC would praise, but in that bizarre "news" report, published March 26th, the CBC shamed these entrepreneurs, repeating the WHO lie that they "won't prevent" the virus and "can be riskier than doing nothing." The only thing that tops that CBC fake news was their report, published back in January, that global warming was to blame[34] for the virus.

China knew full well that the virus was transmitted from person to person — they knew that from their experience in Wuhan, even as they were saying the opposite to the WHO. But it was essential for them to delay, as long as possible, the alarm from waking up the world. While the democracies slept, China's dictatorship — and some of their most loyal ex-pats around the world — had to move quickly to buy up every mask, glove and Lysol wipe in every Costco and Walmart before the west knew what was up. Here's how the *Sydney Morning Herald*[35] described the massive operation, carried out in that country by the Chinese government-owned property company called Greenland

---

32   *https://twitter.com/WHOWPRO/status/1243171683067777024*

33   *https://www.cbc.ca/amp/1.5510998?__twitter_impression=true*

34   *https://www.cbc.ca/news/technology/what-on-earth-newsletter-infectious-disease-climate-change-1.5446356*

35   *https://www.smh.com.au/national/chinese-backed-company-s-mission-to-source-australian-medical-supplies-20200325-p54du8.html*

Holdings, that owns real estate in western cities like Sydney, London, New York — and Toronto, too.

"As the coronavirus took hold in Wuhan earlier this year, staff from the Chinese government-backed global property giant Greenland Group were instructed to put their normal work on hold and source bulk supplies of essential medical items to ship back to China.

"A whistleblower from the company has told the *Herald* it was a worldwide Greenland effort — and the Sydney office was no different, sourcing bulk supplies of surgical masks, thermometers, antibacterial wipes, hand sanitizers, gloves and Panadol [an analgesic] for shipping...

"'Basically all employees, the majority of whom are Chinese, were asked to source whatever medical supplies they could,' one company insider told the *Herald*. This exercise went on for weeks through January and February, he said."

The Australian report said that Greenland Group specifically mentioned that it had bought up medical supplies from Canada: "According to a company newsletter, the Greenland Group sourced 3 million protective masks, 700,000 hazmat suits and 500,000 pairs of protective gloves from 'Australia, Canada, Turkey and other countries.'"

Another report[36] showed China buying massive quantities of "medications, long-life milk, baby formula". It was a worldwide raid, and it had to be done quickly and stealthily, before western governments prohibited the mass export of essential products — or the public realized the peril, and simply bought up the essentials first, or even just pushed up prices.

Those were the sneak attacks in January and February. But as late as April, China's government was officially and publicly banning Canadian companies with factories in China from exporting any masks back to Canada itself. According to the *Wall Street Journal*,[37] "mask maker Medicom Group, based in Montreal, operates three factories in China, including one in Wuhan, where the epidemic emerged. Its

---

36   *https://www.news.com.au/lifestyle/health/health-problems/coronavirus-australia-more-medical-supplies-and-groceries-being-shipped-to-china/news-story/80996 658deb3125807e4d4383b52611f*

37   *https://wsj.com/articles/coronavirus-pressures-supply-chain-for-protective-masks-11583552527...*

supply of materials in China has been diverted by government officials to produce masks for use there, said Kathy Lee, a senior sourcing manager for Medicom."

Is that why Theresa Tam and Patty Hajdu told Canadians not to buy masks? Because the World Health Organization was running a campaign of disinformation and distraction on behalf of the Chinese government?

Or was it — just as likely — that Tam and Hajdu knew Trudeau had just given away our national mask stockpile, and what few were left in Canada were desperately needed for front-line health workers, and lying to Canadians was the best way of trying to save what few masks remained for those on the front lines? Neither answer is reassuring.

The virus came from China. And so does most of the medicine that Canadians (and Americans) buy. According to the U.S. Food and Drug Administration, the U.S. imports more than $150 billion worth of pharmaceuticals and medical devices each year. North America is still where most pharmaceutical research is done; but the manufacturing of medicine has been outsourced, especially to China. According to one study,[38] Chinese factories supply more than 90% of American antibiotics, vitamins and pain medications. The last American factory making key ingredients for penicillin shut down in 2004. Canadian[39] drug manufacturing is shrinking, too.

It's bad enough that relatively low-tech personal protective equipment like cloth face masks and medical gowns is made overwhelmingly in China, as well as more industrially complicated products like N95 masks, also called respirators. Those can be replicated anywhere in a number of months. But rebuilding a deep pharmaceutical supply chain is something that would take years — and the existing supply chain could be a strategic chokehold that a belligerent Chinese dictatorship could use against the west as relations deteriorate further. When you can't buy a face mask, you can make one of your own. Try doing that with Tylenol.

---

38   *https://www.nytimes.com/2020/03/11/business/economy/coronavirus-china-trump-drugs.html*

39   *https://www.ic.gc.ca/eic/site/lsg-pdsv.nsf/eng/h_hn01703.html*

Trump announced his plans[40] to move the factories back, rolling out a US$354 million contract with a Virginia company to produce generic drugs in high-tech factories in the U.S. It's a drop in the bucket compared to the size of the Chinese pharmaceutical industry, but it was enough to raise the attention — and the ire — of China's propaganda media, which bitterly denounced the plan and scoffed at its chances of success.

Whether or not drug factories can successfully return to America remains to be seen; critics wonder whether it's even commercially possible without sustained government support.

Justin Trudeau, by comparison — well, he's investing in pharmaceutical research and development, too. Incredibly, he's sending Canadian research and development dollars too a vaccine project run by the Chinese military.[41] Canada has two roles in the study: to pony up the cash; and to provide the human guinea pigs for the vaccine trials.

The "vaccine candidate" is called Ad5-nCoV, and it is a project of the Institute of Biotechnology of the Academy of Military Medical Sciences — the medical research wing of the People's Liberation Army. Trudeau is literally financing China's military, and couldn't be prouder of it. His bureaucrats boast about the honour: "We are going to get to evaluate it for safety and efficacy in Canada, as is being done already in China, and Canada will now be part of the front-runner story," crowed Roman Szumski, vice-president at Canada's National Research Council (NRC).

Canada will provide the money; but the Chinese company running the project, CanSino, will own all the intellectual property in the vaccine. It's not just foreign aid to a wealthy company in a wealthy country. It's foreign aid to a military contractor, working for the world's second-richest armed forces. According to the NRC, by giving China everything they want, for free, there's a chance China will sell the vaccine to Canada without cutting us off. Not a guarantee, but a

---

40   *https://www.washingtonpost.com/business/2020/05/19/trump-takes-first-step-toward-returning-medical-supply-chains-us/*

41   *https://www.theglobeandmail.com/world/article-national-research-council-strikes-deal-with-china-to-develop-test/*

hope: Canada's involvement "would facilitate guaranteeing supply to Canada," the NRC told the *Globe and Mail.* So it's a definite maybe.

In the meantime, China has big plans for Canada — Trudeau's NRC hopes to supply China's military with human guinea pigs, as soon as September. NRC offices in Halifax will sign up Canadians willing to let the military vaccine be tested on them. With unemployment soaring in Canada, the chance to make a few hundred dollars will likely find takers, even for something as risky as an untested Chinese military vaccine.

Even if it works, why would Canada finance a Chinese vaccine, owned by China? Why test it on Canadians in such a rushed way? And for what — a definite maybe that perhaps China would allow Canadians to use the vaccine, if we're really, really nice to them?

CHAPTER 5

TRUDEAU VERSUS TRUMP

It's hard making decisions in real life about things like viruses, and foreign dictatorships. They don't respond well to Trudeau's traditional tools — speeches, selfies and other gimmicks that seem to work well enough with Canada's journalists. But some things don't happen just from wishing; Trudeau and his cabinet had no experience actually doing things. No wonder Trudeau took a three-month holiday self-hiding at home.

Trump, and to a lesser extent, Canadian premiers like Alberta's Jason Kenney and Ontario's Doug Ford, met the press with their public health advisors; it was obvious that they understood the technical briefings, and were the key decision-makers. It was also evident — especially from Trump, the perpetual deal-maker, and Ford, the long-standing businessman — that a knowledge of business operations was important to get tangible things done in a hurry, whether that was deploying ventilators to hospitals or working the phones to scrounge up emergency masks and other urgent supplies. What a contrast it was between Trudeau and Trump, who often appeared in public with major CEOs, who had just emerged from a meeting where Trump twisted their arms to have them commit to fighting the pandemic. Many did so for free, in a flourish of patriotic goodwill; some, like

General Motors, had to have Trump drop the hammer of the Defense Production Act on them, essentially commandeering their factories to get what he needed.

You could see Trump the deal-maker at work — unafraid to go toe-to-toe with captains of industry, and having the confidence to know how to drive a hard bargain. Trudeau simply never had that experience in life; he really was just a drama teacher and a snowboard instructor until he was wafted up into Parliament on his inheritance and his father's name, failing upward. Neither did Trudeau's inner circle, either in the Prime Minister's Office or cabinet — they were all talkers, not doers. They're more comfortable at a TED Talk or a WE Day pep rally than on a factory floor. So whereas Trump would just pick up the phone and demand that 3M make 39 million N95 masks in 90 days, Trudeau literally just put up "help wanted"-style websites[42] and hoped for the best. To their credit, some Canadian factories retooled on their own — Canada Goose is manufacturing doctors' scrubs; hockey equipment maker Bauer is making doctors' face-masks. But none of it is being led by Trudeau. As he told the Ethics Commissioner, he doesn't actually do any of the business part of things. And it shows.

Trudeau has never really been a "decider". His own father, Pierre, set up the terms of his inheritance so that Justin wouldn't be granted full control of his family's money until he turned 45[43] — which just happened to be a year after he became prime minister. His whole life, decisions were made — and problems were cleaned up — by his father's team of lawyers and accountants. That served him well as a millionaire playboy — but making decisions in a global pandemic takes more than just good accountants. What are the guiding principles for Trudeau's public health experts? If Trudeau listens to them, who do they listen to?

Part of the answer is the World Health Organization, where Tam serves on an oversight committee. The WHO sounds innocuous enough, sounds like one of the few worthwhile agencies at the United

---

42   *https://buyandsell.gc.ca/calling-all-suppliers-help-canada-combat-covid-19*

43   *https://o.canada.com/news/justin-trudeau-admits-that-he-won-the-lottery-with-1-2-million-inheritance-and-successful-speaking-business*

Nations. But it has been relentless colonized by China, who managed to manoeuvre their hand-picked candidate, Tedros Adhanom, into the top job of Director General.

Tedros is a bizarre choice for the position — for one thing, he's the first WHO boss who isn't a medical doctor. He calls himself "Dr. Tedros", but it's just a PhD, not a medical degree. His real experience is as a brutal political boss in his home country of Ethiopia, where he personally helped cover up cholera epidemics, a skill that likely caught the eye of the Chinese Communist Party. One of Tedros's first acts as WHO director general was to appoint Zimbabwe's Robert Mugabe, the notorious and violent human rights abuser, as a "goodwill ambassador" — a move designed to please Mugabe's backers, Communist China. Eventually Tedros blinked — it was just too brazen a political act. But his loyalty to China was back on display in the weeks after the Wuhan virus started to spread, when Tedros flew in for private meetings with the Chinese dictatorship, including with China's president Xi Jinping himself.

Communist China has its operatives around the world — an army of diplomats, millions of foreign students at universities across the west, and most powerfully, the greed of those western capitalists with a scheme for how to get rich quick off the most populous dictatorship in the world, from the NBA to Hollywood to Apple computers. And that's all fine, in a way. Let the "great game" of strategic diplomacy and finance and power continue. But the World Health Organization was supposed to be different — it was supposed to be like the UN itself is supposed to be, a neutral meeting place for all countries in the world, a place to at least try to fulfill higher ideals, and to promote harmony.

Except that countries like China are not the same as countries like Switzerland; to China, international agencies are tools to promote Chinese interests, and to defeat China's enemies. They're not for global harmony and cooperation. It took a couple of months for the world to realize this after the virus outbreak; Donald Trump was one of the first, caustically renaming COVID-19 "the Chinese virus" when Chinese diplomats started circulating conspiracy theories that the pandemic was all engineered by the U.S. military. Trump's blunt style shocked the usual suspects, but within a month, many western democracies were echoing his anger at the Chinese Communist Party.

Boris Johnson, the U.K. prime minister, fell ill with the virus, seriously enough that he was sent to an intensive care unit and the command of the government was temporarily transferred to his deputy, Dominic Raab. Until the virus swept through the U.K., China must have felt optimistic about conquering Britain — Johnson had signed off on Huawei, the massive Chinese technology company, having some involvement in the country's 5G networks. And China was touted as an important trade market for the U.K. post-Brexit. That was abandoned even before Johnson was hospitalized, with senior Conservatives calling for a total overhaul in the relationship.[44] You didn't need to be a tabloid writer on Fleet Street to grasp the drama. As the *Daily Mail*'s headline put it, "Downing Street says China faces a 'reckoning' over their handling of coronavirus and risks becoming a 'pariah state' as Boris Johnson faces pressure to scrap the Huawei deal". Even Emmanuel Macron, the socialist president of France, reached his breaking point[45], calling China's official version of the outbreak a lie. You'd have to be "naive" to believe it, Macron told the *Financial Times*, saying things "happened that we don't know about". Within days, Germany went even further: a newspaper called *Bild* — the largest-circulation newspaper in all of Europe — practically declared war on China, accusing the Communist Party of war crimes and then sending China an "invoice" for €140 billion. It wasn't the official view of Angela Merkel, but it spoke for much of the German establishment. Japan's deputy prime minister wryly said it should be renamed the "China Health Organization". Everyone was inching away from China, politically — not because the virus came from there, but because the Chinese Communist Party covered it up; they lied about its contagiousness; they didn't warn the west or limit travel from Wuhan to the world; and during that period of deception, they scooped up the world's medical protective gear, either to use it, or resell it back to the west at a staggering mark-up. Everyone was walking away except North Korea's Kim Jong-Un — and Canada's Justin Trudeau.

---

44   *https://www.dailymail.co.uk/news/article-8163767/Downing-Street-says-China-faces-reckoning-coronavirus.html*

45   *https://www.bbc.com/news/world-europe-52319462*

In a blow to the WHO — and the United Nations itself — Donald Trump announced in mid-April that the United States was suspending all payments to the health agency pending a review, a suspension he soon made permanent. It was a financial setback to the UN, but more importantly it was a moral setback — a vote of non-confidence by the UN's largest benefactor. But within weeks Trudeau splurged, personally committing Canada to more than make up for any U.S. cutbacks. It wasn't debated in Parliament; it wasn't reviewed by Parliament's budget officer or any committee. It was just announced in a tweet[46] — by Tedros Adhanom himself. "Thank you Justin Trudeau Prime Minister, for the support to WHO during the United Against Coronavirus pledging event and for the contribution of €551M+ to the global Covid-19 response. Together!"

Just like that — a tweet. 551 million euros is worth more than $800 million Canadian dollars, a staggering amount of money at any time, but grossly disproportionate from Canada, more even than was pledged by economic powerhouses like Germany or France. Trudeau promised Canada's entire agriculture industry $252 million in aid to recover from the virus; he gave more than triple that to the WHO — a de facto gift to China, which bizarrely, hadn't paid up itself.

Again, why? Why the submissiveness to China? Why the lavish support for a discredited United Nations agency that has failed abysmally? Why the continuing abuse of anyone or anything critical of the Chinese Communist Party?

For example, in late March, China made a noisy display of sending a small shipment of personal protective equipment (PPE) to Canada, after having vacuumed up many times as much from our country in January and February. The "gift" was nominally from the Bank of China, but of course that's owned by the government, and it was the Chinese embassy that announced it[47] on Twitter. Fewer than three hours later, no-one less than Trudeau's foreign minister, Francois-Philippe Champagne,[48] personally issued a public thank-you in reply to the embassy's press release. Yet, as was the case with Chinese "gifts"

---

46   *https://twitter.com/DrTedros/status/1257311230949126153*

47   *https://twitter.com/ChinaEmbOttawa/status/1243897763508768769*

48   *https://twitter.com/FP_Champagne/status/1243938782522548224*

of PPE to so many other countries, China's shipments to Canada were faulty. Virus-testing kits didn't work; personal protective gear was flawed; name-brand items — like 3M's high quality N95 face masks (that filter out 95% of particles) were simply counterfeits, stamped as 3M but really just shoddy knock-offs. Over a million[49] items were useless — not just useless, but positively dangerous if a front-line health care worker were to rely on them. Trudeau refused repeatedly to criticize China's dangerous goods. But when Taiwan — formally known as the Republic of China, the small democratic island off the coast of China that the Communists have repeatedly sworn to conquer — gave Canada a massive gift of high-quality, high-hygiene masks from its national supply, the ingratitude was stunning. Champagne was repeatedly asked in question period to thank Taiwan by name, but repeatedly refused to even say the word Taiwan, saying he was "very grateful to every nation" that helped. But every nation didn't help; China sent defective and dangerous goods. It was Taiwan, not every nation. But Trudeau didn't dare offend the bullies in Beijing, even when the democrats in Taiwan were saving Canadian lives.

If you can believe it, Champagne is even more submissive to China behind closed doors. Champagne went on Trudeau's February junket overseas, and visited with China's foreign minister, Wang Yi. China's embassy in Ottawa published[50] a "read-out" of the meeting — a summary of the conversation. There was nothing in there about the two Canadian hostages held by China; nothing in there about human rights. But there was this: "Champagne said that Canada admires the outstanding leadership shown by President Xi Jinping and the Chinese government in the fight against the epidemic. China has made important contributions to prevent the spread of the epidemic and is widely appreciated by all parties."

It's shocking. But it's true. Canada — or, more accurately, Trudeau and his government — truly do admire Xi Jinping, even in the midst of the pandemic. They really do "appreciate" China's contributions — even when it's faulty medical gear.

---

49   *https://www.theglobeandmail.com/canada/article-canada-says-one-million-face-masks-from-china-failed-to-meet-proper/*

50   *https://translate.google.com/translate?sl=auto&tl=en&u=http%3A%2F%2Fca.china-embassy.org%2Fchn%2Fzjwl%2Ft1745201.htm*

Diplomats often have to tell white lies — it's one of the subtle meanings of the word "diplomatic". But in Champagne's case, he's not lying, it's really him. In 2017, Champagne appeared on one of China's state-owned TV channels, CGTN,[51] and praised China's Communist system. "In a world of uncertainty, of unpredictability, of questioning about the rules that have been established to govern our trading relationship, Canada, and I would say China, stand out as [a] beacon of stability, predictability, a rule-based system, a very inclusive society." It's hard to believe any Canadian could truly mean that; but Champagne and Trudeau have never given any indication to the contrary. That Champagne would happily spout that obedient propaganda for a Chinese government TV channel — which then used it as proof to their own subjugated citizens that their regime had the world's approval — is particularly worrying. No wonder he refused to even utter the word Taiwan.

Or maybe Champagne's love for China is more personal — as personal as his wallet. In a mandatory financial disclosure to Parliament, Champagne admitted[52] that he currently owes the Bank of China — a government-run bank, controlled by the Communist Party — more than a million dollars in the form of two mortgages for condominiums in London, U.K. Champagne claimed it was totally normal for a Canadian foreign minister to owe seven figures to a foreign country that is locked in a Cold War against us; evidently Justin Trudeau agrees and hasn't ordered Champagne to refinance his mortgages with a less compromising lender. But even Champagne's excuses don't make sense. Champagne borrowed the money when he was a high-flying executive living in London, the world's financial capital, likely home to more banks than any other city in the world. Why on earth would he choose the Bank of China — which is so obscure, that it is ranked 53rd in terms of its size in the London mortgage market? Did the 52 larger banks really reject Champagne, a millionaire businessman? Was the Bank of China giving Champagne a sweetheart deal? Or is Champagne

---

51 *https://www.theglobeandmail.com/politics/article-francois-philippe-champagne-takes-helm-at-department-of-global-affairs/*

52 *https://www.theglobeandmail.com/politics/article-foreign-affairs-minister-has-two-mortgages-with-state-run-bank-of/*

just living his creed — like his boss Trudeau, he just truly, deeply, madly loves Communist China?

To be fair, there is one Liberal cabinet minister who is so hostile to China's Communist Party that it would make even Donald Trump tell him to cool it. He co-authored a newspaper op-ed in April[53] entitled "Xi Jinping's China did this", with the subtitle "The corrupt, criminal regime wasted 40 days blocking information while it crushed domestic dissent and ensured COVID-19 would become a global pandemic".

Alas, the Liberal cabinet minister who wrote that, Irwin Cotler, retired from Parliament in 2015, just as Trudeau became prime minister. Still, Cotler's scorching analysis is worth reading — just to see how far the Liberal Party of Canada has fallen from its traditional position of human rights champion.

Cotler was so outraged by China's misconduct, he even invented a new word for it: an "infodemic", the novel Chinese combination of a pandemic with a Chernobyl-style cover-up.

"The CPC's infodemic — in addition to its intense spinning of solidarity on social media and its framing of a 'people's war against the virus' — was both a deceitful and farcical illusion of a coming together in China. The extent of the CPC's self-promotion and its portrayal of President Xi as a hero ready to save the world — while making Western democracies look grossly incompetent — is as shameful as it is duplicitous."

Cotler didn't just condemn China — he called for democracies to use whatever legal tools were at their disposal to treat Xi Jinping like a kind of war criminal. "The community of democracies must undertake the necessary legal initiatives — be they international tort actions as authorized by treaty law, or the utilization of international bodies, like the International Court of Justice — to underpin the courage and commitment of China's human rights defenders. This is what justice and accountability is all about."

Who knows how many other Liberals believe what Cotler believes? The party used to consider itself the party of human rights — Pierre Trudeau himself regarded the drafting of the Charter of Rights and

---

53   *https://www.timesofisrael.com/criminality-and-corruption-reign-in-xi-pings-china/*

Freedoms as one of his great legacies. But if there are any Liberals left who support freedom and democracy, and oppose authoritarian dictatorships, they know better than to speak up in Justin Trudeau's government — at least when it comes to the tyrants in China.

CHAPTER 6

PANDEMIC RECIPE: OPEN BORDERS AND OPEN SKIES

So when did Trudeau finally stop flights from China, the source of the pandemic? It's a trick question — he still hasn't. See for yourself right now — here's how.

Go to the website of one of the two main airports that receive flights directly from China — Vancouver's airport website is *www. YVR.ca* and Toronto's is *www.TorontoPearson.com*. And click on the arrivals page — you'll see every flight arriving that day and the next day, and the flight number. For example, Xiamen Air continues a regular flight directly from Xiamen, China to Toronto — Flight MF805, it's called. Take that flight number — MF805 — and go to another website, called *www.FlightAware.com*. It's an incredible, real-time visual database that lets you track virtually any airplane in the world just by typing in its flight number, or the route in question. It even tracks private jets based on a tail number, showing you exactly where they are in the air at any given moment.

Xiamen Air is particularly busy, flying directly to Vancouver several times a week — it never stopped. China Eastern Airlines flight MU207 flies directly from Shanghai to Toronto. On any given day, odds are you'll see massive jetliners from any of a half dozen Chinese airlines making their way to Canada. FlightAware even shows you their exact routes, and shows you a picture of the plane.

There hasn't been a day this year when planes haven't come directly to Canada from China. Check for yourself right now.

Did you really think Trudeau had stopped them?

Donald Trump brought in travel restrictions from China on January 31st. He still let American citizens fly home, but he slammed the door on Chinese tourists and others without legal standing — and the Theresa Tams of the United States duly called him a racist. But it took until March 13th for Trudeau's public safety minister, Bill Blair, to announce even the most laughable "screening" for passengers from China and other virus hotspots. "We have enhanced screening measures in place at all international airports, as well as land/rail/marine ports of entry. We are taking the necessary steps to ensure that Canadians are safe in the face of COVID-19," he announced.[54]

Except it simply wasn't true — unless "enhanced screening" simply meant being asked to push a button on a touch-screen kiosk (in English and French only, not Chinese) if you had recently been to Hubei province in China, where Wuhan is. There just wasn't any screening. Airports around the world — including in China and many poor, developing countries — were screening arriving passengers for fevers, using instant infrared thermometers, which work in one second and don't require touching the passenger. Throughout the pandemic, Rebel News reporter David Menzies regularly visited Toronto Pearson arrivals to greet passengers from China and other exotic locations, and not one had ever actually been screened — though quite a few told Menzies they wish they had been. (In mid-June Trudeau finally announced that airports would start taking the temperature of arriving passengers — five months after the first passenger with the virus had flown in.)

Passengers from China arriving in Canada typically land in Vancouver or Toronto, and those cities may in fact be their final destination. But both Air Canada and WestJet have booking arrangements with Chinese airlines, so that arrivals can connect on to other cities that are not served by direct flights from China. Throughout

---

54   *https://twitter.com/billblair/status/1238643631218741248*

the pandemic, passengers landing from China could immediately board domestic Canadian flights to any smaller city, without quarantine.

Under Canada's Constitution, health care is a provincial responsibility; the federal government doesn't run any hospitals. Trudeau really had one job in this pandemic: to close the borders to the virus, much like medieval port cities like Venice and Marseilles would put arriving ships in a 40-day quarantine on little islands just offshore of the mainland until the city's health committee could confirm they didn't have the plague. (That's where the word quarantine comes from — "quaranta giorni" means 40 days in Italian). But whether through laziness or ideological globalism, Trudeau just wouldn't — and he refuses in many ways even now. Exasperated provincial premiers like B.C.'s John Horgan[55] and Alberta's Jason Kenney[56] took matters into their own hands, stationing provincial health officers in federal airports, an assertion of provincial power that would probably have irked Trudeau if he weren't in vacation mode.

---

55   *https://vancouversun.com/news/local-news/covid-19-all-canadians-returning-home-must-have-an-approved-quarantine-plan/*

56   *https://edmonton.ctvnews.ca/i-do-have-concerns-alberta-premier-warns-against-passing-through-airports-1.4854524*

CHAPTER 7

TRUDEAU'S GREAT RECESSION

The virus is on course to kill more than 9,000 Canadians by the end of June. Each death is a tragedy of course; but as late as mid-April, the Liberal government's models[57] projected as many as 50,000 deaths even with strict lock-downs, and a disastrous 350,000 deaths without them. (By contrast, the total number of Canadians killed in both world wars was just over 100,000.) In any given year around 8,000 Canadians die from the regular flu and pneumonia.[58]

Things could still get worse; researchers say the virus has mutated into different strains; and troubling reports from around the world suggest that it's possible to be infected a second time. But so far, the death toll has not been comparable to the plague. In the U.S., the mighty navy hospital ships dispatched by Donald Trump to Los Angeles and New York City remained empty and were sent home. Temporary overflow hospitals built in vacant convention centres have been shut down, without use. In both the U.S. and Canada, thousands

---

57   *https://www.scribd.com/document/455707368/Canada-coronavirus-outbreak-Public-Technical-Briefing-April-9*

58   *https://www150.statcan.gc.ca/t1/tbl1/en/tv.action?pid=1310039401*

of non-emergency surgical procedures were cancelled to free up beds that simply haven't been needed, and across North America, bored nurses and doctors have taken to killing time by recording dance videos on social media.

This is a good thing; and in no way attributable to the sleeping lifeguards who let the virus march right through our airports into our country. But as the death toll models are revised downwards and revised downwards again, other secondary consequences are starting to become more urgent — and possibly even more deadly.

It's a well-researched fact that poverty causes sickness and death. To cite just one study[59] in the American Journal of Public Health, more than 20,000 sets of Swedish twins were tracked for 20-plus years, allowing researchers to compare people with nearly-identical genetics. Twins have the same genetic make-up and similar upbringings. So any difference between them — say, if one twin was working while the other was unemployed — can be studied with a greater certainty that other variables aren't at play. It's conclusive: losing your job makes you sick — and it can kill you, according to the study. "Unemployment was associated with an increased risk of suicide and death from undetermined causes. Low education, personality characteristics, use of sleeping pills or tranquilizers, and serious or long-lasting illness tended to strengthen the association between unemployment and early mortality."

Closer to home, public health scholars in Alberta calculated[60] that during the recent recession in that province, for every percent increase in unemployment, there were approximately 16 suicides. Alberta has just over one tenth of Canada's population. If those same numbers could be extrapolated across Canada, each additional 1% of unemployment would cause approximately 150 suicides nationally. If indeed unemployment from the lock-down really does soar from 5% to approximately 20%, that's more than 2,000 suicides — roughly equal to the entire virus death toll until the end of April.

---

59   *https://www.ncbi.nlm.nih.gov/pmc/articles/PMC1448606/*

60   *https://www.thestar.com/edmonton/2019/09/27/sixteen-more-albertans-die-by-suicide-for-every-one-per-cent-increase-in-unemployment-report-finds.html*

In other words, making an entire country poor can be as deadly as a virus. It's a common sense conclusion but, unlike the spectacular media coverage of an exotic Chinese virus, the death toll of people dying from a collection of poverty-related ailments doesn't get the headlines. Before the pandemic, Canada was teetering on the brink of a national recession; with more than 2 million newly unemployed Canadians and a 9% decline of the economy in a single month, the pandemic recession could be as deep as the Great Recession, and as deadly. Will Trudeau try to "flatten the curve" of unemployment? Or will he continue his controversial policies, even in the face of the crisis? So far, it's not looking good.

The medical crisis had already started to recede by May, but the lockdown was still in effect. Doctors in Northern California were reporting[61] more deaths by suicide than by the virus; a Saskatchewan Indian chief[62] attributed a cluster of ten suicide attempts on his reserve to stress from the virus lockdown. Health Canada predicts that nearly a third of Canadians — 11 million people — will feel "high levels" of stress during the pandemic, with 2 million predicted to show "traumatic levels". There was a massive spike in anti-depression and anti-stress prescriptions.[63] It's not the virus that did it; it's the response to the virus — the social isolation, the forced unemployment, the criminalization of social interaction.

Trudeau is unserious about serious things; and he's serious about childish things — like giving more than $800 million to the WHO in return for a tweet of thanks. Even as Trudeau and his cabinet were unleashing the largest spending spree in Canadian history — purportedly to stimulate the economy and give laid-off workers and businesses some spending money — Trudeau insisted on proceeding with a 50% increase in the carbon tax. It had been scheduled for April 1st — April Fool's Day, by coincidence — and of course it hit the hardest on fuel-intensive industries. That includes the countless

---

61   https://www.washingtonexaminer.com/news/california-doctors-say-theyve-seen-more-deaths-from-suicide-than-coronavirus-since-lockdowns

62   https://www.cbc.ca/news/canada/saskatchewan/waterhen-lake-first-nation-concerns-suicide-attempts-1.5568350

63   https://www.wsj.com/articles/more-people-are-taking-drugs-for-anxiety-and-insomnia-and-doctors-are-worried-11590411600

truckers and delivery personnel who were keeping the country fed and supplied during the lock-down. And the aviation industry, already reeling from so many travel bans. The very people who were hurt the most were the ones Trudeau for whom jacked up the taxes.

Why? The existing carbon tax was bringing in about $2.5 billion/year. Raising it by 50% would only add about a billion dollars in income in the best of times; but with the economy on hold, the increased revenues would surely be modest. And given that, literally a week earlier, Trudeau had pushed through an emergency spending plan for $82 billion, it was clear that he wasn't shy about borrowing. So why did he do it?

If he was shovelling out $82 billion to keep the economy going during the crisis, why did he insist on taking back an addition $1 billion through a tax hike?

Stubbornness was probably a lot of it; Trudeau is genetically incapable of admitting an error, and given that so many Canadian provinces (and Conservative politicians) oppose the carbon tax, Trudeau would feel that he lost face had he backed down. It really wasn't about the money. It was about sending the signal that, to him, the threat of "global warming" was more dire than the threat of a virus. Global warming, male feminism and open borders — those are as close to core beliefs for Trudeau as it gets. They're not beliefs so much as moral talking points, each one of them an opportunity for him to demonstrate how he's morally superior. On March 28th, when the whole country was on lock-down, cooped up in their homes, Trudeau couldn't stop himself from a bit of virtue signalling. He tweeted,[64] "You're already at home tonight, so why not unplug for Earth Hour at 8:30 PM local time? Whatever you do tonight, Stay At Home and Stay Safe."

Millions of Canadians were essentially banned from travel — by plane, bus or car. They were cooped up, and electronics — their cell phones, their Internet, their streaming movies — were their only connection to society and to sanity. Telling people to turn off their power and sit in the dark in their houses — as if Trudeau himself

---

64   *https://twitter.com/JustinTrudeau/status/1244042688904736773*

would do that! — was the 21st century version of Marie Antoinette's "let them eat cake".

The trouble is, Earth Hour is a quirky gimmick that looks woke when it's a virtue-signalling sacrifice for few minutes each year. But when we're all locked in our houses — and two million Canadians are locked out of their jobs — it feels like Earth Hour every hour of every day. It's the leftist dystopia of de-industrialization and de-growth. But like Trudeau's fake personal quarantine, he only talks about it. The rest of Canadians have to live with it.

CHAPTER 8

YOU MUST STAY HOME. BUT MIGRANTS WORKERS CAN TRAVEL

Despite the largest, and most sudden jump in unemployment in Canadian history — far larger than the day after the 1929 stock market crash, for example — Trudeau officially announced plans to bring in more foreign workers as cheap labour. Like his refusal to give up his global warming ideology, he just won't shut the borders, no matter what. He's a United Nations man all the way — he thought he could get enough votes from China and the Third World to put him on a temporary seat of the Security Council. So he wasn't going to abandon the WHO now, or open borders.

So even as Trudeau was borrowing a record-breaking $82 billion to help ease the pain of newly unemployed Canadians, Trudeau was undermining those workers by announcing[65] new, laxer rules of entry for temporary foreign workers — and even pledging $50,000,000 to bring them in.

---

65   *http://www.agr.gc.ca/eng/coronavirus-disease-covid-19-information-for-the-agriculture-and-agri-food-industry/?id=1584732749543*

57

A government briefing note on the subject starts with a perplexing question: "How will the Government address the workforce/labour shortage as a result of the Canadian border being closed?"

What labour shortage? There are two million Canadians looking for work.

"To safeguard the continuity of trade, commerce, health and food security for all Canadians, temporary foreign workers in agriculture, agri-food, seafood processing and other key industries will be allowed to travel to Canada under exemptions being put in place to the air travel restrictions that took effect on March 18."

So Trudeau announced foreign flight bans and quarantines to great fanfare. But two days later he quietly put in loopholes for precisely the people that were meant to be caught in the ban. And for what? So some industrial-scale corporations can save an extra couple of dollars an hour?

Not only did Trudeau grant a mass health exemption to foreign labourers, he loosened the rules to bring them in. "The Government of Canada is also increasing the maximum allowable employment duration for workers in the low-wage stream of the Temporary Foreign Worker Program from 1 to 2 years. This will improve flexibility and reduce the administrative burden for employers, including those in food processing."

Is that the biggest problem Canada has right now? An "administrative burden" for companies bringing in cheap labour? Globalists like to claim that agricultural jobs are work that "Canadians won't do". That's not true; in a way it's never been true, without the missing part of that sentence — it's work Canadians won't do at below minimum wage. But with looming 20% unemployment, even low-wage work, especially in low-skilled or semi-skilled jobs like agriculture, would likely have a line-up of Canadian citizens happy to help.

But even that wasn't enough. In addition to the exemptions and doubling the period that foreign labourers can stay here, Trudeau pledged to cover the costs of putting those foreign workers up in hotels for a quarantine period when they arrive. Millions of Canadians are having trouble paying rent; but Trudeau will cover the cost of housing for foreign migrants. Why the massive subsidy for employers deliberately choosing not to hire Canadians? And why wasn't there a peep out of the "official" party of the left — the NDP — as Canadian workers were being undercut?

A case in point is the massive slaughterhouse in High River, Alberta, owned by Cargill, Incorporated.

Cargill is the largest privately-owned company in the United States, by revenue — over $100 billion a year. It's larger than AT&T. Their massive slaughterhouse in High River, Alberta, processes 4,500 cattle a day. It's a huge operation, employing 2,000 people. Another slaughterhouse in nearby Brooks, Alberta, called JBS Food Canada, is nearly as big. Like Cargill, JBS is a foreign, multi-billion dollar industrial food processor — owned by a Brazilian company.

And both of them are hooked on that cheap, cheap foreign labour.[66] They really are like foreign factories — owned by foreign countries, staffed by foreign workers. Instead of being based in a low-wage country like China, they've simply brought that low-wage corporate model to Canada, in a special bubble where normal labour laws don't apply. That's bad enough if you're an unemployed Canadian looking to be paid a Canadian wage. But there's something else about foreign-staffed, foreign-owned industrial plantations in Canada: for whatever reason, they have become hotbeds of the coronavirus.

In mid-April,[67] when the total count of infected patients in the entire province of Alberta was less than 3,000, fully 484 were linked to the Cargill plant, and 67 from the JBS plant. Alberta's chief medical officer, Dr. Deena Hinshaw, was politically sensitive, but her public remarks made it clear that the infections tore through the plant because the employees were living en masse, as temporary migrant workers often do.

So a couple of multi-billion-dollar foreign companies who refused to hire Canadian workers were shut down because their foreign labourers didn't adopt Alberta style practices. How is that a benefit to Canada's economy — or to Canada's public health?

Why is that the policy? Some factories can threaten to move to low-cost jurisdictions like China if they don't get concessions from

---

66   *https://calgaryherald.com/business/local-business/federal-government-creates-immigration-pilot-program-for-agriculture/*

67   *https://www.theglobeandmail.com/canada/alberta/article-cargill-to-temporarily-close-meat-packing-plant-at-centre-of-alberta/*

Canadian governments — say, a factory making trinkets for Walmart or a dollar store. There really aren't many of those left in North America. But Cargill and JBS can't just relocate to China for cheap labour. They have to be where the cattle are — and the cattle have to be where the ranches are — countless acres of clean, safe countryside, run by trustworthy, ethical Canadian ranchers. The slaughterhouse isn't the key part of the beef industry; the beef is. And lucky for us, Canada's beef industry can't just be relocated overseas. Even if China did have cowboys and ranches, would you be willing to buy a pound of raw, ground beef made in China, and shipped to North America? And the same goes for fruit-pickers in B.C. and Ontario, and fisheries workers in the Atlantic. Multinational processors don't have real leverage — the food is here. So why are Canadians allowing them to continue with predatory labour practices? And why are we covering their extreme health care costs that come with their foreign workers?

But that's all in keeping with the open borders ideology of Trudeau and his ministers. In fact, as recently as February, 2020, Trudeau was still issuing temporary resident visas to travellers from the virus epicentre city of Wuhan, in Hubei Province, China — weeks after the pandemic was known to the world.

According to government documents disclosed to Parliament,[68] as of February 11, 2020, 1,267 passengers arriving at Canadian airports told border officials they had been to Hubei Province in the two weeks prior — and were still let in. Those were the people that Bill Blair, the public safety minister, had said would be subject to "enhanced screening" — simply by using a touch-screen on a kiosk at the airport. So they touched that button — and then walked right into the country.

Incredibly, a whopping 1.9 million Chinese citizens currently hold valid temporary resident visas to travel to Canada. Just 2% are from Wuhan, but that works out to nearly 40,000 people from that virus hotspot with the legal papers to just come on over.

Most Canadians would be startled to hear that our borders are quite that porous. That's a long-term issue for Canada; but even during the

---

68   *https://www.rebelnews.com/exclusive_trudeau_gave_hundreds_of_canadian_ visas_to_wuhan_residents_after_pandemic_began*

pandemic, the Liberal government was issuing new visas — more than 600 to Wuhan after the outbreak.

Back then, Wuhan itself was in lockdown; the Chinese government was publishing propaganda videos of them constructing pop-up hospitals to deal with the virus. Residents of Wuhan were barred from travelling to other Chinese cities, including Beijing and Shanghai. But Canadian officials rubber-stamped visitors from Wuhan by the hundred. As Rebel News reporter Sheila Gunn Reid showed, in the first month of 2020 alone, the Liberals approved 18,200 temporary resident applications for residents of China. 620 were from residents of Wuhan. Tourism accounted for 286 of these approvals. Another 180 visas were granted for the purposes of a "visit".

China itself was terrified of visitors from Wuhan. They were barred from entering other Chinese provinces for any reason at all. But Trudeau was welcoming them by the hundreds just for a "visit". But of course — who wouldn't want to leave a city of death and despair? And the fact that Canada has free health care for all, well, that's just a bonus.

Trudeau's exemptions for cheap foreign labour weren't the only loopholes he quietly added to his so-called ban on foreign travel. After making a tough-talking announcement to keep out American tourists, and anyone with a fever, Trudeau did the same thing he did with the foreign labourers exemption — he sneaked through a legal loophole for another one of his pet projects. In this case: bogus refugees, including those coming in illegally from the United States.

Foreign visitors to Canada did not have their temperature taken on arrival, even when they flew in directly from virus hotspots like China. But at least Trudeau announced that anyone who was observed with a fever and a cough would be turned back — a medical diagnosis that border guards aren't particularly qualified to do, and for which they were not given any equipment, not even a simple thermometer. But at least, in writing, that was his promise.

Except, right after he publicly announced that ban, he amended it through the back door — not in a press conference, but through a cabinet order, adding two massive new exemptions to Canada's quarantine laws.

Canadians had to shelter in place — really, a form of house arrest. No going to restaurants or to the mall. No theatres, no schools, no play dates for the kids, no non-elective surgeries, no non-emergency court hearings. We were all treated like high school kids with a curfew.

But illegal immigrants — including those with a fever and a cough —are specifically exempted from the ban. The exemption came by way of an "order in council". They're just that — orders. Not laws passed by Parliament after a debate and a vote, but an immediate fiat. It's how Trudeau said he wants to run the country for the foreseeable future — just order it to be so, and it's so. No consulting with the public. No input of any sort from the opposition. Just write it, and it's the law.

Take Order in Council number 185,[69] issued on March 26th. It starts pretty well, listing reasons why foreign travellers ought to be restricted from waltzing into the country:

> (a) based on the declaration of a pandemic by the World Health Organization, there is an outbreak of a communicable disease, namely coronavirus disease 2019 (COVID-19), in the majority of foreign countries;
>
> (b) the introduction or spread of the disease would pose an imminent and severe risk to public health in Canada;
>
> (c) the entry of persons into Canada who have recently been in a foreign country may introduce or contribute to the spread of the disease in Canada; and
>
> (d) no reasonable alternatives to prevent the introduction or spread of the disease are available…

That's a pretty convincing rationale. And here's the order — there was similar wording for foreigners arriving on international flights:

> 2 (1) A foreign national is prohibited from entering Canada from the United States if they exhibit the following signs and symptoms:
>
> (a) a fever and cough; or
>
> (b) a fever and breathing difficulties.

So foreigners were specifically banned from entering Canada if they had symptoms. Makes sense. But then Trudeau's order listed people

---

69   *https://orders-in-council.canada.ca/attachment.php?attach=38991&lang=en*

who were exempt. As in — they could come in, even if they did have a fever and a cough or breathing difficulties:

> Subsection (1) does not apply to persons referred to in subsection (2) who seek to enter Canada from the United States for the purpose of making a claim for refugee protection.

Trudeau had made a showy announcement that, finally, the Roxham Road illegal crossing from New York would be closed. Every newspaper in the country carried that news. And indeed it was true, for a few hours. But Trudeau loved that illegal crossing; he loved his virtue-signalling tweet that started the stampede at the border; he loved that it was proof he was the "anti-Trump"; he loved that it was the ultimate proof that he was a globalist who didn't believe in borders, unlike his xenophobic critics. But the pandemic was just too powerful for him to resist; and the contrast between him demanding that law-abiding citizens remain in their homes, while allowing foreign law-breakers to waltz across the border was just too much, even for him.

But once he got the headlines he needed, he reversed course.

If you are a law-abiding American or foreigner who wants to come to Canada on business, or to visit family, you couldn't come in.

But if you literally broke the law, by entering at an illegal border crossing and claiming you're a refugee, you would specifically be allowed in even if you have a cough and a fever.

How? Why?

What virus victim around the world wouldn't then deliberately set out to come to Canada, and to claim refugee status no matter what? Free health care, and a guarantee you won't be deported for years. Trudeau even has hotels booked for you across the Toronto area for free housing — just for refugee claimants.

Trudeau's loophole keeps everyone who's sick out except the liars and law-breakers. As a matter of fact and as a matter of law, it is impossible to walk across the border from the U.S. and be a genuine refugee — America is a safe country, and we even have a kind of international treaty to that effect, called the Safe Third Country Agreement[70]. You just cannot be a refugee from America. But if you

---

70   *https://www.cbsa-asfc.gc.ca/agency-agence/stca-etps-eng.html*

simply say you are, that's enough for Trudeau to let you in — even if you have the virus.

Trudeau passed another stealthy rule by order in council. Order 184,[71] also published on March 26th, created other exemptions to the rule, too. This time, for any foreign citizen with a work permit or a study permit — more than a million exemptions. 150,000[72] of those are Chinese nationals — typically the privileged sons and daughters of Chinese Communist Party officials, or wealthy oligarchs looking to give their children an escape route out of China.

Those foreign students aren't just welcome to come and go. Trudeau actually announced that any foreign students with a Social Insurance Number will be paid the Canada Emergency Response Benefit (CERB) of $500/week,[73] just like a Canadian citizen. In late May, Trudeau went further, waiving the requirement that foreign students need to show proof that they were working, before receiving the CERB — they merely need to "give their word"[74] that they were working to receive the grant, which was designed as a replacement for lost income. And why not? Even prison inmates were receiving the grant[75] and federal bureaucrats were instructed to ignore signs of fraud, and just process the cheques.

It's probably quicker to make a list of the few remaining foreign travellers who can't come to Canada, than the list of exemptions. The purpose of these lengthy orders in council was summarized by government bureaucrats for quick reference in exactly that way: to "broaden the list of foreign nationals who are permitted entry to Canada by any mode of travel." In fact, Trudeau added in a catch-

---

71 *https://orders-in-council.canada.ca/attachment.php?attach=38990&lang=en*

72 *https://www.cicnews.com/2020/02/642000-international-students-canada-now-ranks-3rd-globally-in-foreign-student-attraction-0213763.html*

73 *https://students.ubc.ca/covid19/international-immigration-health-insurance-faq-covid-19*

74 *https://nationalpost.com/news/no-need-to-show-proof-of-work-permit-to-get-cerb-ottawa-tells-temporary-foreign-residents*

75 *https://nationalpost.com/news/do-not-impose-a-stop-pay-federal-workers-ordered-to-ignore-cheating-in-cerb-and-ei-claims*

all: absolutely anyone approved by the ministers of foreign affairs, immigration or public safety can come in.

Canadian citizens are under lock-down. But any foreign citizen with a friend in the Liberal Party can come right in, even if they have a fever and are coughing. Trudeau told the public he's closing the border. But then he told his bureaucrats to open it back up again. He banned travellers before immediately un-banning them.

CHAPTER 9

THE TRUDEAU FAMILY'S LOVE FOR "BASIC DICTATORSHIPS"

U.S. President Donald Trump is obsessed with China — and has been for more than a decade.

Long before the world learned the word "coronavirus", Trump was battling China, whether in trade wars or over the future of North Korea. His promise to the rust belt states was to bring home jobs from China. China, China, China — he talks about China so often, the Internet is full of video compilations of Trump simply saying the word China — or CHY-nah! — over and over again.

But Trudeau is even more obsessed.

It was a shock to many Canadians to hear Trudeau name China as his favourite country in the world.

It was at a ladies-only fundraiser for Trudeau in 2013, when he was Liberal leader but not yet prime minister. An unscripted question from the crowd yielded an unscripted answer — he accidentally told the truth.[76]

"You know, there's a level of of admiration I actually have for China because [of] their basic dictatorship," he said.

There are many things to admire about China — their history, their culture, their art, their people. But to choose the most odious thing about that place, to name the Chinese Communist Party, to actually describe it accurately for what it is — a basic dictatorship — but to name that your favourite part about it?

It was stunning. But it certainly wasn't a mistake. Trudeau caught himself, half-way through his answer — he realized he was too comfortable, too cavalier. He continued: "their basic dictatorship is allowing them to actually turn their economy around on a dime and say 'we need to go green fastest...we need to start investing in solar.'"

That didn't sound much better; did he really admire their ability to steamroll over anything, everything, and just simply command things to happen without any democratic process? Why yes, that's exactly what Trudeau was saying. He was violating the first rule of holes: when you're in a hole, stop digging. So he panicked, and closed this way: "I mean there is a flexibility that I know Stephen Harper must dream about of having a dictatorship that he can do everything he wanted that I find quite interesting."

Except that Trudeau wasn't asked what country he thought Harper would like best. He was asked what country he liked best, and why. And he answered it. They must have been popping champagne corks at the Chinese embassy when they heard that one.

That unique combination of absolute, unvarnished love for China's brutality, matched with a naïveté — imagine thinking that China, the world's largest polluter was some sort of environmental role model! — well, China had never had such a man in their corner before.

Justin Trudeau's father, Pierre, always had a soft spot for tyrants. He was a regular visitor to Cuba; after he retired in 1984, he took his sons on a vacation to Siberia, in the Soviet Union. Trudeau had visited before, including in the 1950s, when it was under Josef Stalin's

---

76   https://www.ctvnews.ca/politics/trudeau-under-fire-for-expressing-admiration-for-china-s-basic-dictatorship-1.1535116

brutal rule. The USSR wasn't just a totalitarian empire back then; it was Canada's sworn enemy. And Siberia itself was home to the gulags, where political prisoners were sent as punishments. But Pierre Trudeau taught his sons that was "the future", as he called it.

Pierre Trudeau was fascinated by dictatorships. He visited China once as prime minister; but he had already visited twice as a private citizen beforehand, including right in the middle of Mao's "Great Leap Forward", a brutal economic program that killed between 20 and 40 million Chinese citizens. Maybe that's the "turn their economy around on a dime" part that Justin Trudeau mentioned.

In other words, Trudeau came by his love for China's dictatorship honestly — he inherited it from his father. So did Trudeau's brother, Alexandre "Sacha" Trudeau, a filmmaker whose works including an anti-American propaganda film produced in cooperation with Iran's dictatorship. Sacha isn't just Trudeau's brother; he was Trudeau's foreign policy advisor on his leadership campaign. And like his dirty deal with Iran's dictatorship, Sacha published a book about China — commissioned by the dictatorship itself, a fact that he boasts about publicly.[77]

That's not a real book then, Sacha. That's a propaganda pamphlet. But as Vladimir Lenin said, there are plenty of "useful idiots" in the west only too happy to work against democracy. Even the title shows the trademark Trudeau loathing for the west: *Barbarian Lost: Travels in the New China*. "I now look at our own freedoms with a little more circumspection and consider some of the irresponsible nature of some of the freedoms we enjoy," writes Sacha.[78] And like his brother, he admires China's basic dictatorship, saying he doesn't believe China "could have come so far so quickly without the unity and organizational power."[79]

Just by sheer coincidence, Sacha's book came out around the time Justin Trudeau was on his first official visit to China as prime minister.

---

77   https://www.cpac.ca/en/programs/tete-a-tete/episodes/49034493/

78   https://ottawamagazine.com/arts-and-culture/alexandre-trudeaus-memoir-is-as-a-barbarian-lost-in-the-biggest-human-story/

79   https://themontrealeronline.com/2016/11/alexandre-trudeau/

Sacha said,[80] "he read it a week before he left for China and he told me it helped him get up to speed in what to think and feel about China." No wonder Trudeau was so subservient when he got there — it's the Trudeau family tradition to bow and scrape to China's dictators.

The funny thing is, China doesn't seem to be impressed with it. When Donald Trump, one of the harshest critics of China, visited the country, they rolled out the red carpet for him and, according to the New York Times,[81] the Chinese establishment gave him two nicknames: Donald the Strong, and Uncle Trump — both names carrying some respect, even admiration.

Trudeau's nickname was "Little Potato" — a play on words, but also a diminishment. That didn't seem to dawn on Chrystia Freeland, who was the foreign minister at the time, who boasted to the world just how proud she was that Trudeau was given that nickname.

80   *https://ca.news.yahoo.com/qa-with-alexandre-trudeau-on-his-china-book-his-154706884.html*

81   *https://www.nytimes.com/2017/11/09/world/asia/trump-china-fans.html*

CHAPTER 10

CHINA BUYS THE LIBERAL PARTY

While the Trudeau boys and Freeland were star-struck by a nickname and flattery, the real decision-makers in the Liberal government got down to business. Like Trudeau told the Ethics Commissioner, he doesn't really do any actual work. He leaves that to the smarter guys and the harder-working guys. And in the case of Canada-China relations, Trudeau hired every China lobbyist and corporate shill he could find. More than any other issue — from taxes to trade to health care — the single-most pronounced characteristic of any given Trudeau staffer is that they are part of the China lobby.

Even before Trudeau was sworn in, China lobbyists were appointed to the highest offices of his government. Trudeau appointed Peter Harder to lead his transition team — perhaps the single most important position, as it was Harder's job to fill hundreds of posts within the government. Harder's job before that? he ran the Canada-China Business Council, the chief pro-China lobby group in Canada.

The entire foreign policy team was in a contest with itself to see who could be more pro-China. In early 2017, Trudeau appointed John McCallum as Canada's ambassador to China, who famously testified that his approach to any and all Chinese relations was simply,[82] "more, more, more". Not more for Canada; not getting more from China. Just simply more — more of whatever China would offer him. He would take anything, really. He'd say anything. Sometimes it was hard to tell: was he Canada's ambassador to China — or China's ambassador to Canada?

As an MP, McCallum accepted countless free trips to China from their government — $73,000 worth, while he was in opposition. Apparently that's legal, as long as McCallum disclosed them, which he did. The Chinese government must have known he was a good investment for them to pour such resources into him.

After Trudeau brought the Liberals back to power, McCallum remarked that Canada had "more in common" with China under Xi Jinping than it did with the United States under Donald Trump. He just couldn't stop loving China, even after that dictatorship seized two Canadian hostages, Michael Spavor and Michael Kovrig, in retaliation for Canada arresting Chinese telecom executive Meng Wanzhou, the chief financial officer of Huawei, for financial crimes.

Meng may or may not be guilty; she has had access to the finest lawyers, and lives a life of luxury in Vancouver while she fights her extradition to the U.S. Independent courts will decide. The arrest — really, the kidnapping — of the two Michaels is anything but a proper legal process, and Chinese diplomats have expressly called it a tit-for-tat. It's an outrage — it's China's basic dictatorship. That ought to be evident to anyone; but even if McCallum couldn't see it, his sole mission as ambassador was to take Canada's side. But he just couldn't quit loving China, and giving them more, more, more.

At a press conference in Toronto with the Chinese-language media, McCallum publicly said he thought Meng had a strong case; and he suggested that the whole thing was simply a political intrigue or a bargaining chip to Donald Trump.

There is no way that a senior ambassador — and former cabinet minister — had an organized press conference, in front of the Chinese-language press, without the full knowledge and involvement

---

82   *https://www.theglobeandmail.com/politics/article-ottawas-man-in-china-mccallum-an-ambassador-like-no-other/*

of Trudeau's office. Whether they simply underestimated the public shock, or never thought the news would leak out from the Chinese press to the mainstream press, is unclear. Trudeau simply couldn't keep McCallum — he had painted Trudeau into a corner, so he had to be fired. But is there any doubt that, until the moment he was sacked, McCallum was China's most loyal asset in the Canadian embassy?

Peter Harder was a key China appointment for Trudeau — because he was in charge of so many other hires. And John McCallum was the most important appointment, because he was the ambassador. But China's influence in the Trudeau government is strong precisely because it is so pervasive — being pro-Beijing is an unquestionable act of faith for a Trudeau Liberal, as much as being a feminist.

Take Yuen Pau Woo — appointed to the Senate by Trudeau and made leader of the Liberal-aligned "independent" Senators group. He has a long history of supporting China, and like Harder, before he joined Parliament he was the head of a pro-China lobby group too, the Asia-Pacific Foundation. His speeches[83] in Canada's Parliament sound like they could be given in China's National People's Congress, including a bizarre tirade in support of China's attempts to annex more territory — a provocation that has been deemed illegal by international tribunals. Woo suggested that for Canada to merely condemn China's actions could in fact trigger a war — an insane comment for anyone to make; but, like McCallum's obeisance to China and Tam's submission to the WHO, it begs the question: whose side is Woo on?

There's a tone-deafness among Trudeau's Liberals — it's like they are surrounded by pro-Beijing groupthink, and don't even know how extreme they look, because they're all doing it. Take Mary Ng, another one of Trudeau's gender-quota cabinet ministers. She visited China last year on a junket, despite China holding the two Canadians hostage. And she and Peter Harder posed for a photo,[84] smiling ear-to-ear at an ice cream shop in Beijing.

Is it heartless to go on a pub crawl-style party through China, and tweet selfies about it, while two Canadian hostages remain in a Chinese

83   *https://vancouversun.com/news/local-news/trudeaus-b-c-senate-appointee-a-beijing-apologist-mp-charges/*

84   *https://ipolitics.ca/2019/07/03/ministers-tweet-during-china-trip-criticized-as-out-of-touch/*

prison? Probably; but if everyone from the prime minister and his brother on down are doing it, if the ambassador and the Liberal boss in the Senate are doing it, then that's obviously the culture in the Liberal Party — not only is it acceptable, it's the way to get ahead.

It's natural to be pro-China in the Liberal Party. Much more natural than being pro-America. In a recent TV interview about whether or not to allow Huawei to build Canada's 5G networks, Navdeep Bains, Trudeau's "Innovation" Minister, defiantly told Trudeau's CBC state broadcaster that he "refused to be bullied" by the United States and their worries about security breaches.

Huawei — China's leading telecom company — wants to build the world's 5G (fifth generation) networks. But the company's ties to the Chinese Communist Party, along with a law that requires all Chinese tech companies to allow the dictatorship unfettered access to their data, makes that a strategic security risk for any country. Both the Obama and Trump administrations have pleaded with Canada not to allow China to install Canada's networks. But Huawei knows Trudeau better than most. They watched him mooch a free vacation from the Aga Khan and then try to cover it up. Trudeau is already as sympathetic to China as could be; but if there was any doubt about it, the way to his heart is through his wallet. So Huawei has poured money into Trudeau's political machinery.

Corporate donations to political parties aren't allowed in Canada. But the Liberal Party has an in-house "think tank" called Canada 2020. And for years, Huawei has been backing up the Brinks truck to Canada 2020, and dumping cash all over it. Unlike donations to a party, it's not limited to a maximum donation. It's not even disclosed. For years, Huawei ensured that its logo was prominently displayed on Canada 2020's website — until China kidnapped the two Canadian hostages, and even the Liberals knew it would be tacky to show loyalty to the hostage-takers just for a few pieces of silver. (If it's even possible, Hockey Night in Canada has lower standards — like so much of the professional sports industry, they're only too eager to take Chinese blood money.)

But while Huawei no longer flies its flag over Canada 2020, it has hired[85] one of Canada 2020's founders, Tim Barber, whose Twitter biography describes himself as a "Liberal sycophant". Other Huawei lobbyists, political consultants and spin doctors include Liberal speechwriters Scott Reid and Scott Feschuk; former Liberal MP Joe Jordan; former Liberal candidate Scott Bradley; Paul Martin advisor Morgan Elliott; and of course Jean Chretien himself, who has publicly demanded that Trudeau abandon the extradition of Huawei's CFO, Meng Wanzhou. The fact that Chretien is now a full-time China lobbyist — and his son in law, Andre Desmarais, is Canada's largest investor in China — somehow manages to be omitted in the press reports of his Sinophilia. Since the pandemic, Huawei's colonization of the Liberal Party has become even more valuable, since the Chinese Communist Party itself is so widely discredited. Having a high tech company lobby for China helps distract from that fact that they're simply carrying on diplomacy by means of business — China's most successful military weapon in the 21st century.

Chinese corporations like Huawei don't donate money directly to the Liberal Party of Canada — it's illegal for any corporation, even Canadian companies, to do that. But there are so many dark money accounts in Trudeauland, it hardly matters. Take the Trudeau Foundation — a massive slush fund for not only the Trudeau family, but for Liberal Party hangers-on. That's where Trudeau would send Chinese millionaires looking to make donations in exchange for favours, since it was all off-the-books. One happy donor just happened to be Zhang Bin, a member of China's "National Committee of the Chinese People Political Consultative Conference". That's a part of the Chinese dictatorship whose closest comparison would probably be the Canadian Senate. Zhang happily spread a million dollars around Montreal, including $200,000 that wound up in the Trudeau Foundation, and a staggering $50,000 for a statue of Pierre Trudeau.[86] It's possible that a Chinese Communist Party boss had a true affection for the Trudeau family — the Trudeaus certainly have an affection for

---

85   *https://cartt.ca/huawei-loads-up-on-liberal-influence-with-bluesky-hire/*

86   *https://www.cbc.ca/news/politics/chinese-fundraiser-trudeau-statue-1.3863266*

China — but Zhang's official biography[87] makes it clear, his goal is "enhancing the global influence" of China. What exactly did Zhang seek to influence? And how would we even know how he went about it?

No-one who has watched the grifting by Trudeau and his family can be genuinely surprised that they accept dark money from foreign dictators. But Trudeau has invented something completely new: having a sitting Canadian cabinet minister working for the Chinese Communist Party, on an actual committee "in support of the national five-year plans." As in: Trudeau is returning the favour to his Chinese dictator friends.

The China Council for International Cooperation on Environment and Development[88] is not a bi-lateral organization that serves both China and Canada, like a chamber of commerce or a diplomatic group. It's an actual office of the Chinese government. And Canada's Environment Minister, Jonathan Wilkinson, actually works for it, as did his predecessor, Catherine McKenna. The council's membership list is obviously dominated by Chinese bureaucrats. There are a few ex-pats who come from the world of the United Nations. But the only sitting politician from another country, who goes to work for the government of China, is Trudeau's environment minister.

Here's an excerpt from the official[89] "about us" charter of the council, wholly owned by the Chinese dictatorship: "CCICED will provide policy analysis and recommendations, technical support, best practice experience and early warning in support of the national five-year plans and China's goal of building a moderately well-off (Xiaokang) society."

It's not a Canada-China trade group. It's got nothing to do with Canada, other than we pay for it, and we actually make Canadian cabinet ministers do it. No other country actually embeds its cabinet ministers in a foreign government, and tasks them with making Chinese people better off — no mention of our own country. It's nuts.

---

87   *Enhancing the global influence*

88   *http://www.cciced.net/cciceden/ABOUTUS/Membership/Membership/*

89   *http://www.cciced.net/cciceden/ABOUTUS/Charter/*

Even more incredible, Canadian taxpayers cover the cost[90] of this — we pay $1.6 million dollars a year, to the Chinese government, for the privilege of sitting on their council, to help them meet their five-year plans.

How did that ever come to be? And how on earth did it continue, despite China seizing Canadian hostages, stealing Canadian trade secrets, boycotting Canadian agriculture, and lying to us about the virus?

Canada's submissiveness to China is deeper than Trudeau lets on; in fact, sometimes Canadians only learn about the latest humiliation that Trudeau has consented to when a Chinese propaganda outlet brags about it. Take the staggering news[91] in October, 2019 — on the eve of the virus outbreak — that Canada had participated in a Chinese military competition.

This wasn't just some amateur sports competition. It was specifically a military sports competition. But the *Globe and Mail* headline that broke the story in Canada was the strangest part: "Beijing says Canadian military participation at Chinese sports competition more proof it's not losing global support".

Beijing says so? Is that how we had to find out about this? Absolutely. The Canadian military sent Canadian soldiers over to China to have fun, to play some sports, engage in a little bonhomie, to normalize that country, to give them moral and political cover. Trudeau and Defence Minister Harjit Sajjan surely knew it couldn't remain a secret — sending hundreds of Canadians to China for a mini-Olympics was going to be news, eventually. But there were no press releases or tweets about it from Canada.

Beijing knew exactly what they were doing. This wasn't about sports or even about military matters. "Beijing's embassy in Canada says the fact the Canadian military just sent a 'big delegation' to a sporting competition in China is more evidence the Asian power is not losing friends," reported the *Globe and Mail*. China was bragging, using Canada's submissiveness as proof that it's doing just fine. In fact,

---

90   *https://www.canada.ca/en/environment-climate-change/services/climate-change/call-statement-intent-china-council.html*

91   *https://www.theglobeandmail.com/politics/article-canadian-military-sends-athletic-team-to-beijing-sports-competition/*

it was a sort of "checkmate" move by Beijing; the week before, the Globe and Mail published a column called "How China Loses Friends and Alienates People," arguing that China's bullying of Hong Kong democracy activists would cost Beijing support. Instead of arguing to the contrary, Beijing just proved it: if China was so isolated, why was the Canadian government trying so hard to please them?

So China broke the news — they told the world Trudeau and Sajjan's secret, by outing them on the Chinese embassy's website:[92] "The 7th CISM Military World Game in Wuhan, China, attended by 9,308 military athletes from 109 countries, including a big delegation from Canada, speaks volumes in this regard." (Amazingly, the military games were in the very city in China that was ground zero for the epidemic just weeks later.)

Canada had sent a huge delegation — 114 athletes and 57 coaches and support staff. Normally, that's the sort of thing that you brag about, tweet about, issue press releases and photos about. One hundred and seventy-one people flying to a country for a sporting event is not quite an Olympic-sized delegation, but it's huge, many millions of dollars. It's not something we do regularly for even our own NATO allies; and earlier in the year, Trudeau cancelled the 2019 NATO Air Force war games held in Cold Lake, Alberta, called Maple Flag — the Canadian equivalent to the Top Gun program. There was no money for that; but there was plenty of money to send 171 military men and women to Wuhan.

Harjit Sajjan himself should know better, but like his boss Trudeau, he loves China. He even attended a celebration for the 70th anniversary of the Chinese Communist Party — right in the middle of the 2019 Canadian election campaign. Not a celebration of China the country, or China the people. It was cheering for the Communist dictators.[93] That's demoralizing enough for the family of the two Michaels; for democracy activists in the Chinese-Canadian community. But what about to Sajjan's own troops?

---

92   *http://ca.china-embassy.org/eng/sgxw/t1710894.htm*

93   *https://nationalpost.com/news/canada/defence-minister-sajjan-ripped-for-attending-gala-honouring-chinese-communist-party-anniversary*

Trudeau treats Canadian soldiers poorly and Canadian veterans even worse. But veterans of China's People's Liberation Army are flourishing in Canada — and they even have their own version of the Legion — incorporated in Canada as the Canada Chinese Veterans Society.[94] They dress up[95] in Chinese military uniforms, sing songs about vanquishing Communism's enemies, and generally act out China's vision of world domination. It's only surprising that Sajjan hasn't attended one of their galas, too — although, like the secret military mission to Wuhan, perhaps we'll need to find out about it from the Chinese embassy, when it suits them to prove a point.

It's unthinkable that China would allow military veterans from foreign countries have similar celebrations in their territory; but so much of the Canada-Chinese relationship is unthinkable in the usual terms of diplomatic relations: reciprocity. Like all human relationships, international diplomacy is a two-way street, whether it comes to trade, taxes or even just symbolic good wishes. Things couldn't be more one-sided in the Canada-China relationship; and even the economic and human devastation of the Chinese coronavirus doesn't seem to have shaken Justin Trudeau and his government out of that sleepwalk.

94   *https://www.ic.gc.ca/app/scr/cc/CorporationsCanada/fdrlCrpDtls. html?corpId=10932507&V_TOKEN=1571343617462&crpNm= veterans&crpNmbr=&bsNmbr=*

95   *https://nationalpost.com/news/canadian-veterans-of-peoples-liberation-army-form-association-sing-of-chinas-martial-glory*

CHAPTER 11

WHAT DO ORDINARY CANADIANS THINK OF CHINA?

Trudeau's unshakeable love for the Communist Party of China is so hard to explain, it suggests there could be a real risk of what the Soviets called "Kompromat" — compromising material used to extort western politicians. But while Trudeau continues to admire China's dictatorship, ordinary Canadians have had enough. A series of polls done during the pandemic show that China — the dictatorship, not the ethnicity — is one of the most despised governments in the world, in the eyes of Canadians.

The Angus Reid Institute, one of Canada's most venerable pollsters, surveyed[96] public opinion on China and found that only 14% of Canadians have a favourable view of that country, a new low, falling in half from the 29% who had a favourable opinion last year. More than 85% of Canadians say the Chinese dictatorship has not told the truth about what happened in its own country about the virus.

---

96   *http://angusreid.org/covid19-china/*

Only 11% of Canadians say Canada should focus efforts on increasing trade with China — a number that was 40% when Trudeau first took office. Four out of five Canadians want Huawei banned from building 5G infrastructure.

Canadians of every partisan stripe are against China. Only 1% of Conservative Party supporters are "very favourable" towards China — the same as among Trudeau's own Liberals. And even the hard-left NDP is deeply unfavourable towards it — even more so than Liberals.

Interestingly, while Trudeau, Tam and Hajdu have slavishly adhered to the WHO's pro-China messaging, ordinary Canadians don't buy it. Even amongst Liberal supporters, only 12% believe China is telling the truth.

Perhaps the most hopeful statistic in the Angus Reid poll is that Canadians, despite being bombarded by pro-Chinese propaganda, both from abroad and from our own media, still put Canadian cultural values ahead of pure profit. So many industries, from the movie business to professional sports teams, have decided to put their ethics on hold to pursue China's massive market. But not ordinary Canadians. Back in January of 2019, right after China took the two Michaels hostage, 38% of Canadians said trade was the most important part of the relationship, and 62% said human rights and the rule of law was. Now, after the pandemic, those numbers are even more lopsided, 24% to 76%.

Of course, Canadians could have both, if we were discussing a democracy — that's why we love the U.S. and the U.K., and even the EU. But if China is forcing us to choose — and indeed they are — Canadians will choose Canadian values.

Another Canadian poll[97] by B.C.'s Research Co., finds similar grassroots hostility to China — 72% of Canadians demanding that China "take responsibility for its role in the COVID-19 outbreak", with just 18% disagreeing. But that poll asked a radical hypothetical question: should the Government of Canada "consider launching legal action against the People's Republic of China on account of the COVID-19 outbreak"?

---

97   *https://researchco.ca/wp-content/uploads/2020/05/Tables_Poli_COVID19_CAN_19May2020.pdf*

It's not common to sue countries. Our system of law recognizies "sovereign immunity" — if you start to think of all the nuisance suits that the rest of the world would bring against Canada, it's easy see why. But it's not unprecedented, especially when there's a rogue regime at play. And the question can be used as a proxy for other legal remedies like sanctions or taking away trade privileges from China. So it's a bit radical, but not in the realm of fantasy.

So far, just 20% of Canadians are strongly for such a lawsuit with another 11% moderately for it — a total of 31%. It's not a majority, but it's a sizeable chunk. Research Co. found 22% of Canadians are against the idea, 27% strongly against it — a total of 49%. Not quite half, but still more than those who want to sue China.

But the very question would have been unthinkable just a year ago, wouldn't it? Canadians are so stunned by China's misconduct that they're open to dramatic solutions to deal with China — a total reset of Trudeau's pro-China policy. That's very interesting; if the Conservative Party were ever to form government, they might even consider it — according to the poll, 42% of Conservative voters support the idea of a lawsuit, and only 38% oppose it.

Taken altogether, that's a dramatic change in Canadian public opinion — and it mirrors the change in other countries, as documented by Pew Research, a major public opinion think tank in the U.S. It's no surprise that U.S. public opinion has hardened against China: Donald Trump has been sparring with China long before he became president, and he has been waging a brutal trade war against them for years; rhetorically it's the country he criticizes the most. So it's understandable that Americans have turned on China — they've had the world's leading China critic as their president for nearly four years. But in Canada, it's been the opposite — we've had the world's leading Chinese sycophant for five years, someone who meekly sends them care packages of face masks, even as they continue to hold Canadian hostages. It's a sign of good taste and discernment that Canadians have come to oppose China despite having no clear public champion for that position in our country.

CHAPTER 12

CAN WE WIN THE CHINESE COLD WAR?

So what should we do with China? Not the country; not the people. But the Chinese Communist Party. The exact origin of the virus is unknown. But what we know without a shadow of a doubt is that, however the virus came about, China's Communist Party deliberately covered up the facts, arrested doctors who were trying to warn about it, lied to the world, including the World Health Organization, which they got to radiate their lies, and engaged in outrageous bad faith conduct, vacuuming up the world's medical supplies for two months while pretending everything was fine.

Perhaps it's time to stop thinking about China as a trading partner. (It's not really a partnership when Canada buys $75 billion/year from them, and they buy just $23 billion in return from us.) And they're certainly not an ally. They are much more than just a competitor, as their illegal trade practices constantly show, and their industrial espionage proves. Lest we forget, Canada once had a world-leading high-tech company called Nortel — with nearly 100,000 worldwide employees, and a stock market value of nearly half a trillion dollars.[98] It was our Apple, our Google — until Chinese hackers stole everything and drove it to bankruptcy. For a full decade, Huawei simply ripped off the intellectual property developed and paid for by Canadians. And now they come to build our 5G networks.

China is not a business partner. We do buy things from enemies — we buy oil from OPEC dictatorships. But no-one pretends they are dear friends and partners and allies. There are other analogies that fit better, and give us a template for how to respond to China. Apartheid South Africa, perhaps — how the world denormalized and put sanctions on South Africa for its policies of Apartheid. It was an odious, racist system to be sure, but its cruelty was inwardly focused — it didn't also kill hundreds of thousands of people around the world like the Wuhan virus. For moral reasons, the west put economic sanctions on South Africa, and more importantly, it was turned into a pariah state.

Why isn't China treated as a pariah? The Chinese Communist Party is heartily racist in their words and deeds. It is ethnically cleansing Tibet, it has imprisoned millions of Uyghur Muslims, it murders adherents of the Falun Gong and it abuses Christians, just to name the more famous examples. Even during the virus crisis, China has turned against the thousands of African labourers who live and work in China, evicting them from apartments, banning them from stores and restaurants, based on one bizarre official conspiracy theory that the virus originates in Africa.

So how should we treat the Chinese Communist Party — like we treated the Nazis? It fits; Mao Zedong killed between 50 and 80 million souls — more than Hitler did. But Hitler attacked the world; Mao murdered his own people, mainly.

Perhaps the best analogy is our Cold War stance towards the Soviet Union. China, like the USSR was, is large, and nuclear armed. You can't attack it. You can't ignore it. But you can denormalize it, speak truth to power about it, and make sure you are never dependent on it.

---

98   *https://business.financialpost.com/legal-post/the-fate-of-once-mighty-nortels-last-billions-lies-in-the-hands-of-two-men*

Canada can undo our favours to it. We can recognize Taiwan as an independent country — something, to our deep discredit, that hasn't been done by the free world in a generation.

We can encourage our companies to leave China. Not just like Trump; like Japan, too. Japan is taking billions of dollars from their pandemic stimulus program,[99] offering to pay its companies to bring home their factories from China. It's cheaper than the alternative — when you factor in the economic devastation that our connection with China has wrought.

We need to address the reasons why companies left for China in the first place. A factory is a factory; it's capital-intensive machines. Was it something else that drove factories to China besides just cheap labour? Likely too much red tape in Canada, the U.S. and Europe; too much government hassle, too much litigation, too much environmentalism. Whatever it is, it can't be worse than the economic and health Chernobyl that China inflicted on us and the world. Let's bring our factories home — with carrots if possible, but sticks too. Tariffs on anything made in China — and use that money to help pay for the reshoring of other companies. Is it really good public policy that we are held hostage by China for most of our medicines? More than 90% of antibiotics sold in North America are made in China.[100] Put aside concerns of product integrity — if we give a hostile dictatorship our supply chain, why would we be surprised if they decide to yank that chain from time to time?

We have to clean out the Chinese Communist Party's influence in global institutions — or, since that is likely impossible, simply create new institutions for democracies. Why does China have a veto at the UN? Why is China on influential panels[101] of the UN's human rights council? Why does China, the virus infector, run the World Health Organization?

---

99 *https://www.scmp.com/news/asia/east-asia/article/3079126/japan-pay-firms-leave-china-relocate-production-elsewhere-part*

100 *https://www.cfr.org/blog/us-dependence-pharmaceutical-products-china*

101 *https://thediplomat.com/2020/04/china-appointed-to-influential-un-human-rights-council-panel/*

In addition to their control over the WHO, China now runs more UN agencies than any other country[102] — the International Civil Aviation Organization, the Food and Agriculture Organization, the UN Industrial Development Organization, and the International Telecommunication Union. Each of those agencies has a strategic use for China as a weapon — to promote its own interests and punish its enemies. Why would any Canadian — or American, Brit, Australian or other free citizen of the world — accept the 21ˢᵗ century's equivalent to the Soviet Union running those organizations?

Why not defund the UN and the rest of the globalist institutions infiltrated by China? China has the world's largest foreign currency reserves, they can surely pay for them. And why not start new institutions for liberal democracies? Not useless talk shops that simply demonize the democracies and run cover for the dictatorships. Let the UN move its headquarters to Wuhan, and give a new, democratic institution its prestigious New York office space.

And let's do what Ronald Reagan and Margaret Thatcher and Pope John Paul II did to the Soviets. Let's speak truth to power; let's call them out; let's denormalize them; and let's quietly support dissidents. Reagan and the west supported the Polish Solidarnosc labour union that helped undo the Soviet Union. The Pope himself visited Poland and had a massive outdoor mass, with more than a million Poles, and he told them: "be not afraid". And so they weren't.

Let's do that sort of thing to China. Let's unhook ourselves from them industrially; financially; let's root them out. Let's send home many of the 150,000 Chinese nationals at our Canadian universities — at least the ones who are activists for the Chinese Communist Party. It's worse than you think. Last year, when a Tibetan-Canadian woman was elected as student body president at the University of Toronto in Scarborough, 10,000 students signed a vicious petition against her, purely based on her ethnicity and her support for Tibet.[103] That kind of abuse of Chinese ethnic minorities and democracy activists in Canada isn't new — but so far, Canadian authorities have been

---

102   *https://twitter.com/HillelNeuer/status/1253612698761400321*

103   *https://freetibet.org/news-media/na/over-10000-sign-petition-rejecting-tibetan-university-student-president-canada*

loath to criticize it. Why? Even during the pandemic, China hasn't relented. When Huawei's Meng Wanzhou had a key court appearance in Vancouver in May, 2020, Chinese consulate staff were on hand to videotape the faces of every anti-China protester gathered outside — undoubtedly running the images through a facial recognition program, and building a database of "enemies". That sort of intimidation isn't always subtle — in a major report[104] released in March, 2020, Amnesty International documented "continued incidents of digital attacks, phone harassment, in-person monitoring of individuals in Canada, harassment and intimidation at demonstrations, harassment of family members in China, and interference with freedom of assembly and media." As just one example, a mob of 100 pro-Beijing activists surrounded a Vancouver church where a peaceful prayer meeting was being held in support of Hong Kong democracy activists. Police had to be called to escort the frightened worshippers out of the church.[105] Amnesty's report is full of literally dozens of cases like this. It needs to stop; but how?

This will surely be hard to do, because we have gone so far the wrong way. So much in our lives is made in China, from our computers to our cell phones, to half the cheap household items at Walmart and Canadian Tire. That's the main difference between denormalizing China and denormalizing the former Soviet Union — we weren't buying $75 billion of goods from the Russians each year.

Everything we like is made in China. But the pandemic was made in China, too. And the cover-up was made in China. The danger still comes from China. Let's at least start acting like it — and maybe one day, like Poland, the Chinese people will be free.

---

104   *https://www.amnesty.ca/sites/default/files/Canadian%20Coalition%20on%20Human%20Rights%20in%20China%20-%20Harassment%20Report%20Update%20-%20Final%20Version.pdf*

105   *https://www.thestar.com/vancouver/2019/08/20/christian-group-says-its-religious-rights-were-violated-when-pro-china-supporters-surrounded-church.html*

CONCLUSION

As this book goes to press, the virus is long past its worst peak in Canada. The terrifying scenarios of mass deaths just didn't happen, other than the notable exception of certain seniors homes. Some provinces did not have a single fatality; in most parts of the country, it was no worse than the annual flu season.

The response by public health authorities, including the overreaction of shutting down the entire economy and locking people in their homes, will surely be reviewed at great length. Were those cures worse than the disease?

But the pandemic revealed a much deeper problem in Canada: the dangerous political connections that Justin Trudeau and his Liberal Party have forged with the Communist Party of China, ties that remain strong today.

That's the real China virus — and even after COVID-19 is relegated to the history books, that's the real danger to Canadians.